monday

tuesday

wednesday

thursday

friday

weeknights with giada

Monica —

xo

weeknights with giada

quick and simple recipes to revamp dinner

Giada De Laurentiis

Clarkson Potter/Publishers

New York

Copyright © 2012 by Giada De Laurentiis
Photographs copyright © 2012 by Amy Neunsinger

Published in the United States by Clarkson Potter/Publishers,
an imprint of the Crown Publishing Group, a division of
Random House, Inc., New York.
www.crownpublishing.com
www.clarksonpotter.com

CLARKSON POTTER is a trademark and POTTER with colophon
is a registered trademark of Random House, Inc.

Library of Congress Cataloging-in-Publication Data
De Laurentiis, Giada.
Weeknights with Giada / [by Giada De Laurentiis].—1st ed.
Includes index.
1. Cooking.   2. Cookbooks.   I. Title.
TX643.D43   2012
641.5—dc23   2011018531

ISBN 978-0-307-45102-6
eISBN 978-0-307-95322-3

Printed in China

Design by Marysarah Quinn
Jacket photograph by Amy Neunsinger

10 9 8 7 6 5 4 3 2 1

First Edition

For everyone who comes home after a long day
and wonders what to cook for dinner

contents

introduction

I come from a long line of great cooks and eaters, and I've always felt at home in the kitchen. In fact, it's one of my favorite places to be, and I count my blessings every day that I get to do what I love for a living. I could happily wile away hours shopping at a local market and then cooking a three-course meal for dinner.

Except that these days—other than for a special occasion or gathering—I have a good reason not to because there's something I enjoy even more.

In just the past year or two, my daughter, Jade, who turns four this year, started eating real dinners. Those first couple years were such a whirlwind of baby food, different meal times, naps, and early bedtimes that I couldn't have imagined the day my husband, Todd, Jade, and I would all sit down together to eat a real dinner! Yet here we are, finally, and I couldn't be more thrilled. I look forward to our dinners and to spending as much time together at the table as possible.

I think back to when I was a child and how important it was for my family to gather each night for dinner. We had family traditions—like getting to order our favorite dinner for our birthdays—but we always ate the same meal together; there was no way my mom was going to make four separate dishes for each of my brothers, my sister, and me!

I definitely don't have time anymore to cook for hours every day—not if I want to spend time at the table with Todd and Jade. But I still love food and cooking and want to eat a nice dinner! So I've really shaken up my weeknight repertoire to include only dishes that I can pull together after a full day. All of these recipes (except the sides and desserts) make main-course servings. And they can all be accomplished in under an hour—with most on the table much faster than that: Rustic Vegetable and Polenta Soup (page 31), a hearty soul-warming one-pot dish, cooks in under twenty minutes; Lemony White Bean, Tuna, and Arugula Salad (page 43) is a great meal that's quickly assembled from pantry and fridge essentials; Ham, Gruyère, and Apple Panini (page 61) are gooey, cheesy, crunchy, and delicious in ten to fifteen minutes; Spicy Linguine with Clams and Mussels (page 90) is a fifteen-minute-or-less spectacular pasta; and you can't beat Grilled Sirloin Steaks with Pepper and Caper Salsa (page 111), which are also ready in just fifteen minutes.

I've kept some of the traditions my family had while I was growing up and have added many of my own. I cook one meal for the whole family. I feel like I won the lottery with Jade because she eats pretty much everything. Part of it is definitely luck, but I have also worked at it. If Jade doesn't eat carrots one night, or the next time we have them, for example, I change it. I'll puree them with yams (see page 193) or

serve them raw as a finger food with a dipping sauce. I chop them up and add them with peas and corn to Turkey and Pancetta Pot Pies (page 128); Jade loves digging for treasures beneath a buttery, flaky crust. If all that fails, carrots may go away for a while, but I'll try to bring them back in the not-so-distant future. You've got to keep mixing things up so dinnertime isn't a chore or something to get through but, rather, something everyone looks forward to!

Once a week, we have "breakfast for dinner," a new tradition in our house. Jade gets such a kick out of having pancakes for dinner! And I feel great about serving them, especially when they've got almond paste mixed in (see page 170), which makes them taste amazing— and also makes them more substantial. Extras freeze well and I just pop them in the toaster oven for a quick after-school snack for Jade. I always have eggs in the fridge, and combined with fresh veggies or fruits, I can whip up Eggs Florentine (page 172) or Peach and Cherry Frittata (page 171), a surprisingly addictive savory-sweet combo.

Sometimes I fix sandwiches for dinner, and we'll take them with us for a picnic out on the patio or down by the beach. Mediterranean Halibut Sandwiches (page 62), bursting with sun-dried tomatoes and fresh herbs, are so perfect for this, and just close enough to tuna salad to keep kids on board, too. And the change of venue is enough to keep things interesting!

If friends or my sister, Eloisa, and her son, Julian, are coming over, Todd might grill rib-eye steaks while I make a smoky arrabiata sauce (see page 114). Or, I might really surprise them and make something they don't expect from me, like Sweet and Spicy Greek Meatballs (page 141), which Jade adores and make a great school lunch the next day; or a Thai dish—one of Todd's favorite cuisines—such as Thai Turkey Lettuce Cups (page 147), which are great hot or at room temp. Side dishes, like Sautéed Kale, Mushrooms, and Cranberries

(page 207) or Roasted Zucchini and Summer Squash with Mint (page 201), are a great way to stretch a meal to serve a few extra last-minute guests at the table.

In an effort to eat healthfully and mindfully, we've started having meatless Mondays in our house, which has coincided with my discovering my new favorite ingredient, quinoa. It's got a nuttier texture than rice and is higher in protein, which is great for vegetarian-friendly meals, like quinoa with purple Peruvian potatoes, green peas, black olives, fresh herbs, lime juice, and a little agave (see recipe, page 151). There are lots of options in these pages to add or subtract ingredients to suit your taste: Orzo with Smoky Tomato Vinaigrette (page 101) can have ground beef mixed into it (Todd is a fan of this version), or you can take out the cheese from Couscous with Watermelon, Watercress, and Feta Cheese (page 37) to make a refreshing vegan dish.

One thing that never changes is my desire for a little something sweet at the end of the meal. I like to bake a batch of Peanut Butter Cookies with Blackberry Jam (page 215) on the weekend so I can dip into the cookie jar each night. I've also upped my arsenal of dump-and-stir loaf cake and cupcake recipes, such as Chocolate Mascarpone Pound Cake (page 220) and Mini Pumpkin Cupcakes (page 219), for when last-minute bake sales or class treats pop up. When all else fails, Gingerbread Affogato (page 230)—combining ice cream, coffee, and warming spices—is a great dish to turn to when I haven't thought of dessert in advance.

But I really do try to plan ahead so weeknights are stress-free. I always make sure I have my go-to ingredients on hand—the ones that help me speed up prep work but don't sacrifice any flavor. For example, I love artichokes but there's no way I could spend time cleaning fresh ones on a weeknight! Frozen artichoke hearts taste great and mean I can still eat one of my favorite ingredients anytime.

Store-bought pizza dough lets me bake pizza at home anytime. I have been eating more brown rice these days than white, but it can take a while to cook, so I stock store-bought pre-cooked, which is ready to go and tastes great in Ricotta Cheese, Lentil, and Brown Rice Rolls (page 102). Pasta is an obvious fast dinner and there are now so many great types of pastas out there, including different kinds of whole-grain and gluten-free ones. Try different brands to see what you and your family like. Brown rice and quinoa (and corn) pastas, which are gluten free, are great options, as are lentil and spelt pastas. I also make sure I have canned beans and lentils, some great jarred marinara sauce, and some fresh and frozen fruits and vegetables in my kitchen. Then I can pick up a rotisserie chicken if need be on the drive home and I'm good to go!

This is what weeknights look like in my house. I hope these recipes inspire you and your family to gather around the table (or picnic blanket!) for some fantastic dinners—and, most important, a whole lot of fun. *Buon appetito!*

xo

Giada

soups & salads

soups & salads

Beef and **Cannellini Bean**
Minestrone

Creamy **Sweet Potato**
and Rosemary Soup

Asparagus Soup
with Herbed Goat Cheese

Shrimp and **Sausage
Cioppino**

Rustic **Vegetable** and
Polenta Soup

Jalapeño and Cherry Tomato Gazpacho

Creamy Cauliflower Soup with Bacon

Caramelized Onion, Chicken, and Grapefruit Salad

Couscous with Watermelon, Watercress, and Feta Cheese

Grilled California-Style Chopped Salad with Shrimp

Brussels Sprout Leaf Salad

Potato, Orange, and Arugula Salad

Lemony White Bean, Tuna, and Arugula Salad

Roasted Salmon, Snap Pea, and Cucumber Salad

Chicken, Bibb, and Arugula Salad with Raspberry Vinaigrette

beef and cannellini bean minestrone

A traditional Italian minestrone has a variety of veggies in a delicious broth. For a complete meal in a bowl, I like to add ground beef. Serve this with some crusty bread to dip as you go or to soak up the last bit at the bottom of the bowl!

serves 4 to 6

3 tablespoons olive oil
1 medium yellow onion, finely diced
1 large carrot, peeled and cut into ¼-inch pieces
1 celery rib, cut into ¼-inch pieces

Kosher salt and freshly ground black pepper
8 ounces (92% lean) ground beef
3 garlic cloves, minced
1 tablespoon tomato paste
4 cups low-sodium beef broth

1 (28-ounce) can diced tomatoes
1 (15-ounce) can cannellini beans, rinsed and drained
1 dried bay leaf
½ cup grated Parmesan cheese

In a large saucepan or Dutch oven, heat the oil over medium heat. Add the onion, carrot, and celery and season with ½ teaspoon salt and ¼ teaspoon pepper. Cook, stirring frequently, for 5 minutes, until the vegetables are soft. Increase the heat to high and add the ground beef and garlic. Season with ½ teaspoon salt and ¼ teaspoon pepper. Cook for 6 to 7 minutes, until the beef is browned and cooked through.

Stir in the tomato paste until combined. Add the broth, tomatoes, beans, and bay leaf. Bring to a boil. Reduce the heat so that the mixture simmers and cook until the liquid has reduced by half, about 30 minutes. Remove the bay leaf and discard. Season to taste with salt and pepper.

Ladle the soup into bowls and garnish with the Parmesan cheese.

creamy sweet potato and rosemary soup

This is one of my new favorite go-to soups, especially in the winter when the weather isn't really cooperating. I've served this as a casual meal by the fireplace with Todd and Jade, and we've even packed it into a thermos to take with us ice-skating at the rink in downtown Los Angeles.

serves 4 to 6

3 tablespoons unsalted butter, at room temperature

3 tablespoons olive oil

3 large or 6 small shallots, thinly sliced

2 to 3 garlic cloves, minced

Kosher salt and freshly ground black pepper

2 pounds (2 to 3) sweet potatoes, peeled and cut into ½-inch pieces

2 (6-inch-long) stems fresh rosemary

6 cups low-sodium chicken broth

½ cup (4 ounces) mascarpone cheese, at room temperature

3 tablespoons maple syrup

In an 8-quart stockpot, melt the butter and oil together over medium-high heat. Add the shallots and garlic and season with ½ teaspoon salt and ¼ teaspoon pepper. Cook for 3 to 4 minutes, until soft. Add the sweet potatoes, rosemary, and chicken broth. Season with ½ teaspoon salt and ¼ teaspoon pepper. Bring the mixture to a boil, reduce the heat, and simmer until the sweet potatoes are very tender, 20 to 25 minutes.

Turn off the heat and remove the rosemary stems. Using an immersion blender (or in batches in a food processor or blender), blend the mixture until smooth and thick. Whisk in the mascarpone cheese and maple syrup until smooth. Season to taste with salt and pepper. Ladle the soup into bowls and serve.

asparagus soup with herbed goat cheese

Make this soup for a light meal when you want something healthy. The little marbles of goat cheese create a creamy swirl as they melt into the hot soup.

serves 4 to 6

½ cup (4 ounces) fresh goat cheese, at room temperature
½ cup plus 2 tablespoons chopped fresh basil leaves
Kosher salt and freshly ground black pepper

Vegetable oil cooking spray
2 tablespoons unsalted butter, at room temperature
1 large leek (white and pale green part only), thinly sliced

4 cups low-sodium chicken broth
2 pounds medium asparagus, trimmed and cut into 1-inch pieces

Line a small baking sheet with parchment or waxed paper. Using a fork, in a small bowl, combine the goat cheese and 2 tablespoons of the basil until smooth. Season with ½ teaspoon salt and ¼ teaspoon pepper, or to taste. Spray a ½-ounce cookie scoop or a round tablespoon measure with vegetable oil. Scoop the goat cheese into balls and place on the prepared baking sheet. Refrigerate while you make the soup.

In a Dutch oven or large saucepan, heat the butter over medium heat. Add the leek and cook, stirring constantly until softened, 3 to 4 minutes. Add the broth, asparagus, and remaining ½ cup basil and season with ½ teaspoon salt and ¼ teaspoon pepper. Increase the heat to high and bring to a boil. Reduce the heat so that the mixture simmers and cook for about 15 minutes, until the asparagus is tender.

Using an immersion blender (or in batches in a food processor or blender), blend the soup until smooth. Season to taste with salt and pepper. Ladle the soup into shallow bowls and garnish with the herbed goat cheese.

shrimp and sausage cioppino

Surf and turf in a bowl! I've taken a classic Italian seafood stew and given it a twist by adding chunks of spicy Italian sausage to the sweet sautéed fennel, creamy cannellini beans, and shrimp in a rich tomato broth. If you prefer less heat, go for sweet sausage instead of the spicy.

serves 4

¼ cup olive oil
1 large fennel bulb, trimmed and chopped into ½-inch pieces
4 garlic cloves, smashed and peeled
2 large or 4 small shallots, chopped
Kosher salt and freshly ground black pepper

1 pound spicy Italian turkey sausage links, casings removed
2 cups dry white wine, such as Pinot Grigio
¼ cup tomato paste
3 cups low-sodium chicken broth
1 dried bay leaf

1 pound peeled and deveined large shrimp
1 (15-ounce) can cannellini beans, rinsed and drained
1 cup fresh basil leaves, chopped
1 tablespoon chopped fresh thyme leaves
Crusty bread

In a Dutch oven or large saucepan, heat the oil over medium-high heat. Add the fennel, garlic, shallots, ½ teaspoon salt, and ¼ teaspoon pepper. Cook, stirring occasionally, until the vegetables are slightly softened, about 4 minutes. Add the sausage and break into ½-inch pieces with a wooden spoon. Cook until brown, about 5 minutes.

Add the wine and scrape up the browned bits that cling to the bottom of the pan with the wooden spoon. Stir in the tomato paste, chicken broth, and bay leaf. Bring to a simmer, cover, and cook over medium-low heat for 10 minutes.

Uncover the pan and add the shrimp, beans, basil, and thyme. Simmer, uncovered, until the shrimp is pink and cooked through, about 4 minutes.

Remove the bay leaf and discard. Season to taste with salt and pepper. Ladle the cioppino into soup bowls and serve with crusty bread.

rustic vegetable and polenta soup

In Northern Italy, polenta, or boiled cornmeal, is arguably the staple starch—more so than pasta. I've created a rustic, peasant-style soup with instant polenta and simple fresh vegetables for a dinnertime warming of the body and soul.

serves 4

3 tablespoons olive oil
1 medium yellow onion, chopped
2 medium carrots, peeled and cut into ½-inch pieces
Kosher salt and freshly ground black pepper
3 garlic cloves, minced

2 medium zucchini, chopped into ½-inch pieces
3 plum tomatoes, chopped into ½-inch pieces
2 tablespoons chopped fresh thyme leaves
2 tablespoons chopped fresh flat-leaf parsley leaves

4 cups low-sodium chicken broth
⅓ cup instant polenta, such as Gia Russa
3 tablespoons unsalted butter, at room temperature

In a large, heavy saucepan, heat the oil over medium-high heat. Add the onion, carrots, 1 tablespoon salt, and 1 teaspoon pepper. Cook, stirring frequently, until the onion begins to brown, about 6 minutes. Add the garlic, zucchini, tomatoes, thyme, and parsley. Cook for 3 minutes.

Pour in the broth and bring the mixture to a boil. Slowly stir in the polenta, adding it in a fine stream, and cook until the soup thickens and the vegetables are tender, about 8 minutes.

Stir in the butter and season to taste with salt and pepper. Ladle into soup bowls and serve.

jalapeño and cherry tomato gazpacho

Living in Southern California, where we're lucky to have warm weather almost year-round (except for some iffy winter months), cool gazpacho is a refreshing standby in our house. This version takes the traditional Spanish soup of pureed raw tomatoes and vegetables and adds an Italian touch—polenta croutons, which make for a more filling dish.

serves 4

gazpacho

1 pound (about 4 cups) ripe cherry tomatoes

2 medium cucumbers, peeled and chopped, or 4 Persian cucumbers, chopped

1 jalapeño chile, stemmed, seeded, and coarsely chopped

1 serrano chile, stemmed, seeded, and coarsely chopped

1 large or 2 small shallots, coarsely chopped

1 garlic clove, smashed and peeled

2 tablespoons apple cider vinegar

2 to 3 teaspoons hot sauce, such as Tabasco, to taste

Kosher salt

⅓ cup grated Parmesan cheese (optional)

croutons

Vegetable oil, for frying

½ (18-ounce) tube store-bought pre-cooked polenta, cut into ½-inch cubes

for the gazpacho: Puree the tomatoes, cucumbers, chiles, shallot, garlic, vinegar, hot sauce, and 1½ teaspoons salt in a blender until smooth. Taste and add additional salt, if needed. Pour the gazpacho into a bowl and set into a larger bowl filled with ice water. Stir occasionally until chilled, 10 to 15 minutes.

for the croutons: While the soup is chilling, in a large, heavy-bottomed saucepan, pour in enough oil to fill the pan by 1 inch. Heat over medium heat until a deep-frying thermometer inserted in the oil reaches 375°F. (If you don't have a thermometer, a cube of bread will brown in the oil in about 3 minutes.) Working in batches, carefully add the polenta cubes and fry, stirring occasionally to keep the cubes separated, until golden brown, about 2 minutes. Drain on paper towels.

Ladle the gazpacho into four soup bowls, top with the polenta croutons, and sprinkle with Parmesan cheese, if desired.

creamy cauliflower soup with bacon

Cauliflower, when cooked, is so buttery and creamy that it makes for a fantastically rich and filling but light soup. There is no actual cream in this recipe! With the addition of crispy herbed croutons and bacon, you get a dose of healthy with a touch of splurge. Serve this hot if you're in a hurry or make it in advance and chill it. It's great either way.

serves 4

10 to 12 strips (about 1 pound) thick-cut applewood smoked bacon
3 tablespoons unsalted butter, at room temperature
1 large or 2 small shallots, thinly sliced

2 celery ribs, chopped
Kosher salt and freshly ground black pepper
2 garlic cloves, chopped
1 (1½-pound) head cauliflower, cut into 1-inch pieces

1 tablespoon chopped fresh thyme leaves
4 cups low-sodium chicken broth
8 ounces store-bought plain croutons, or crusty bread

Place an oven rack in the center of the oven. Preheat the oven to 400°F.

Arrange the bacon in a single layer on a rimmed baking sheet. Bake for 15 to 17 minutes, until brown and crispy. Drain the bacon on paper towels. When cool enough to handle, chop into ½-inch pieces.

In a large saucepan or Dutch oven, melt the butter over medium-high heat. Add the shallots, celery, 1 teaspoon salt, and ¼ teaspoon pepper. Cook until soft, about 4 minutes. Add the garlic and cook until aromatic, about 30 seconds. Stir in the cauliflower, thyme, and broth and bring to a boil. Reduce the heat so that the mixture simmers, cover the pan, and cook until the vegetables are tender, 20 to 25 minutes.

Using an immersion blender (or in batches in a food processor or blender), blend the soup until smooth. Season to taste with salt and pepper. Ladle the soup into bowls and garnish with the bacon and croutons, or serve with crusty bread.

caramelized onion, chicken, and grapefruit salad

This recipe was inspired by my friend Maxine Greenspan. She makes a fantastic version of this sweet and savory salad with segments of pink grapefruit and tender, caramelized onions. (Make a double batch of the onions and store them in the fridge; they're great on sandwiches and pizzas or to top grilled meat.) To make this a meal, I like to add shredded store-bought rotisserie chicken.

serves 4

caramelized onions

3 tablespoons olive oil
2 medium yellow onions, very thinly sliced
1 tablespoon balsamic vinegar
½ teaspoon kosher salt
¼ teaspoon freshly ground black pepper

salad

2 pink grapefruits
1 head of romaine lettuce, thinly sliced or torn into 1-inch pieces
1 large fennel bulb, trimmed and thinly sliced
1 small cucumber, peeled, seeded, and thinly sliced
3 scallions, finely sliced

1 tablespoon chopped fresh thyme
2 tablespoons red wine vinegar
2 tablespoons fresh lemon juice
1 teaspoon honey
Kosher salt and freshly ground black pepper
¼ cup extra-virgin olive oil
2 rotisserie chicken breasts, shredded (about 2½ cups)

for the caramelized onions: In a large skillet, heat the oil over medium heat. Add the onions, balsamic vinegar, salt, and pepper. Cook, stirring occasionally, until the onions are deep golden brown, about 20 minutes. Set aside to cool.

for the salad: While the onions are cooking, peel each grapefruit and then slice crosswise into wheels. Put them in a large salad bowl. Add the lettuce, fennel, cucumber, scallions, and thyme.

In a small bowl, whisk together the red wine vinegar, lemon juice, honey, ½ teaspoon salt, and ¼ teaspoon pepper. Slowly whisk in the olive oil until blended.

Add the dressing and chicken to the salad and toss until all the ingredients are coated. Season to taste with salt and pepper. Arrange the caramelized onions on top and serve.

couscous with watermelon, watercress, and feta cheese

This is the perfect summer salad; it's so beautiful and refreshing. Sweet ripened watermelon pairs with tangy, salty feta cheese and crunchy watercress. I add Israeli couscous, which is nice and plump, to turn this into a meal.

serves 4

Kosher salt and freshly ground
   black pepper
1 cup Israeli couscous
Grated zest and juice of
   2 lemons

¼ cup extra-virgin olive oil
2 tablespoons honey
1 (4-pound) piece watermelon,
   rind removed, flesh cut into
   ½-inch cubes

2 (4-ounce) blocks feta cheese,
   cut into ½-inch cubes
2 packed cups (2 ounces)
   watercress or arugula

In a medium saucepan, bring 3 cups of water and 1 teaspoon salt to a boil over medium-high heat. Stir in the couscous and reduce the heat so that the mixture simmers. Cover the pan and cook for 8 to 10 minutes, until the couscous is tender. Drain and set aside to cool for 15 minutes.

In a salad bowl, whisk together the lemon zest, lemon juice, olive oil, honey, 1 teaspoon salt, and ½ teaspoon pepper. Add the cooled couscous, watermelon, feta, and watercress. Gently toss until all the ingredients are combined. Season to taste with salt and pepper. Serve immediately.

grilled california-style chopped salad with shrimp

California is home to the chopped salad, and many versions of it. I'm a huge fan of these colorful salads at both lunch and dinnertime because they're chock-full of fresh ingredients that fill you up without weighing you down.

serves 4

1 head of romaine lettuce, trimmed and halved lengthwise
1 ear of corn, husk and silk removed
2 medium zucchini, halved lengthwise
6 colossal or 12 extra-large shrimp, peeled and deveined

Olive oil, for drizzling
Kosher salt and freshly ground black pepper
½ head of butter lettuce, torn
2 medium tomatoes, chopped into ½-inch pieces
1 avocado, peeled, seeded, and cut into ½-inch cubes

3 tablespoons fresh lemon juice
3 tablespoons extra-virgin olive oil
1½ tablespoons agave nectar or honey
2 cups store-bought tortilla strips, such as Mission Restaurant Style

Place a grill pan over medium-high heat or preheat a gas or charcoal grill.

Drizzle the romaine lettuce, corn, zucchini, and shrimp with olive oil. Season with 1½ teaspoons salt and ½ teaspoon pepper. Grill the romaine, turning occasionally, until crisp-tender and browned in spots, about 2 minutes. Grill the corn and zucchini for 2 minutes on all sides until crisp-tender. Grill the shrimp for 2 to 3 minutes on each side, until the meat is opaque and cooked through.

Coarsely chop the grilled lettuce and place in a large salad bowl. Using a sharp knife, remove the kernels from the corn and add to the salad bowl. Chop the zucchini into ½-inch pieces and add to the bowl. Cut the shrimp into ½-inch pieces and add to the bowl. Add the butter lettuce, tomatoes, and avocado to the bowl.

In a small bowl, whisk together the lemon juice, extra-virgin olive oil, agave nectar, ½ teaspoon salt, and ¼ teaspoon pepper until smooth.

Pour the dressing over the salad and toss until all the ingredients are coated. Season to taste with salt and pepper. Garnish with tortilla strips and serve.

brussels sprout leaf salad

This is the most time-consuming recipe in the book in terms of prep, but I love it so much I just had to include it. You can prepare the Brussels sprouts (even blanch them ahead) on the weekend, drain them well, and refrigerate until ready to eat. Tossed with some arugula, endive, toasted almonds, and a light lemon dressing, this is a simple yet substantial vegetarian dish.

serves 4

1½ pounds Brussels sprouts
2 packed cups (2 ounces) baby
   arugula
1 Belgian endive, cut into
   ½-inch pieces

⅓ cup sliced almonds, toasted
   (see Cook's Note)
¼ cup extra-virgin olive oil
¼ cup fresh lemon juice (from
   1 large lemon)

Kosher salt and freshly ground
   black pepper
⅓ cup grated pecorino romano
   cheese

Bring a large saucepan of salted water to a boil over medium-high heat. Have ready a bowl filled halfway with ice water.

Meanwhile, if you have time, use a small paring knife to separate the leaves from the Brussels sprouts. (Reserve cores for another use.) Otherwise, you can simply cut the Brussels sprouts in quarters, which is faster. Add the Brussels sprouts to the boiling water, cooking leaves for 1 minute and quarters for 2 minutes. Drain and transfer to the bowl of iced water. Once cool, drain well in a colander.

Combine the Brussels sprouts, arugula, endive, and almonds in a salad bowl.

In a small bowl, whisk together the olive oil and lemon juice until smooth. Season with ½ teaspoon salt and ¼ teaspoon pepper.

Add the dressing to the salad and toss together. Season to taste with salt and pepper. Sprinkle with the cheese and serve.

cook's note

To toast almonds, arrange in a single layer on a baking sheet. Bake in a preheated 350°F oven for 6 to 8 minutes, until lightly toasted. Cool completely before using.

potato, orange, and arugula salad

Potatoes are a staple in my household—Todd loves them—so I wanted to come up with a potato salad that wasn't heavy or coated in mayonnaise. This salad keeps the potato as the star ingredient while the citrus gives it some life. Gorgonzola adds a pop of flavor, and the toasted walnuts supply a welcome crunch.

serves 4 to 6

Vegetable oil cooking spray
1½ pounds baby potatoes, halved
¼ cup plus 2 tablespoons extra-virgin olive oil
Kosher salt and freshly ground black pepper

2 medium oranges
2 packed cups (2 ounces) arugula
½ cup (2 ounces) crumbled gorgonzola cheese

⅓ cup chopped walnuts, toasted (see Cook's Note)
3 tablespoons fresh orange juice
1 tablespoon champagne vinegar

Place an oven rack in the upper third of the oven. Preheat the oven to 400°F.

Spray a heavy baking sheet with vegetable oil. Toss the potatoes and ¼ cup of the olive oil in a medium bowl until coated. Arrange in a single layer on the prepared baking sheet and season with 1 teaspoon salt and ½ teaspoon pepper. Roast for 20 minutes. Turn the potatoes over and continue to roast for 15 to 20 minutes longer, until golden. Set aside to cool for 15 minutes.

Meanwhile, grate the zest from one of the oranges; reserve 1 tablespoon for the dressing. Peel the oranges and slice crosswise into wheels. Put the wheels in a large salad bowl. Add the arugula, gorgonzola cheese, walnuts, and cooled potatoes.

In a small bowl, whisk together the remaining 2 tablespoons olive oil, the orange juice, the vinegar, and the reserved orange zest until smooth. Season with ½ teaspoon salt and ¼ teaspoon pepper.

Add the dressing to the potato mixture and toss until coated. Season to taste with salt and pepper, and serve.

cook's note

To toast walnuts, arrange in a single layer on a baking sheet. Bake in a preheated 350°F oven for 6 to 8 minutes, until lightly toasted. Cool completely before using.

lemony white bean, tuna, and arugula salad

Keeping your kitchen stocked with staples such as canned tuna and white beans, capers, onions, lemons, and greens will help you to get together a great salad like this in no time after a long day. The maple syrup rounds out the lemon and olive oil dressing and helps bring out the best in the ingredients here.

serves 4 to 6

6 packed cups (6 ounces) arugula
1 (15-ounce) can cannellini beans, rinsed and drained
½ small red onion, thinly sliced
3 tablespoons capers, rinsed and drained

1 teaspoon grated lemon zest
3 tablespoons fresh lemon juice (from 1 large lemon)
1 tablespoon maple syrup
3 tablespoons extra-virgin olive oil

Kosher salt and freshly ground black pepper
1 (12-ounce) can of tuna in olive oil, flaked with a fork into ½-inch chunks

In a large salad bowl, combine the arugula, beans, red onion, and capers.

In a small bowl, whisk together the lemon zest, juice, and maple syrup. Slowly whisk in the oil until smooth. Season with ½ teaspoon salt and ¼ teaspoon pepper.

Pour the dressing over the salad and toss well until coated. Add the tuna and gently toss to combine. Season to taste with salt and pepper, and serve.

roasted salmon, snap pea, and cucumber salad

I've prepared this salad for a girlfriends' brunch, as well as for dinner for myself when Todd is traveling (which means I don't have to think about serving a meal that will fill him up). I love that this simple salad has such personality, with its freshness, color, and healthful ingredients.

serves 4

1 pound sugar snap peas, trimmed
2 small Persian cucumbers, unpeeled, thinly sliced
1 cup (about ½ pint) cherry or grape tomatoes, halved

¼ cup chopped fresh dill
½ cup extra-virgin olive oil
Grated zest of 1 large lemon
¼ cup fresh lemon juice (from 1 large lemon)

¾ teaspoon kosher salt
½ teaspoon freshly ground black pepper
1 (14.75-ounce) can of boneless, skinless pink salmon, drained

Bring a large saucepan of salted water to a boil over high heat. Add the snap peas and cook until vibrant green, 1 to 2 minutes (see Cook's Note). Drain and transfer to a bowl of iced water to cool, about 2 minutes. Drain and put in a salad bowl. Add the cucumbers, tomatoes, and dill.

In a small bowl, whisk together the olive oil, lemon zest, lemon juice, salt, and pepper until smooth.

Using a fork, flake the salmon into ¾-inch pieces and add to the salad bowl. Pour the dressing over the salad and toss until coated.

cook's note

As an alternative to boiling, the snap peas can be lightly steamed for 2 minutes.

chicken, bibb, and arugula salad with raspberry vinaigrette

When you're not sure what to do with chicken sitting in the fridge, here's an option. You can also use leftover turkey, which makes this a perfect post-Thanksgiving salad, especially with the toasted pumpkin seeds. The recipe yields a good amount of dressing, but I like to store the extra in the fridge to have on hand for quick salads.

serves 4 to 6

½ cup unsweetened frozen
    raspberries, thawed
¼ cup extra-virgin olive oil
2 tablespoons fresh lemon juice
1 tablespoon honey
½ teaspoon kosher salt

¼ teaspoon freshly ground
    black pepper
1 large head of butter or Bibb
    lettuce, torn into 1-inch
    pieces (about 4 cups)
4 packed cups (4 ounces)
    arugula

¾ cup shelled pumpkin seeds,
    toasted (see Cook's Notes)
2 rotisserie chicken breasts (see
    Cook's Notes), thinly sliced
    (about 2 cups)

Puree the raspberries, olive oil, lemon juice, honey, salt, and pepper in a blender until smooth.

In a large salad bowl, mix the lettuce, arugula, and pumpkin seeds. Add the vinaigrette and toss until all the ingredients are coated. Thinly slice the chicken on the diagonal and arrange on top of the salad.

cook's notes

To toast the pumpkin seeds, arrange in a single layer on a baking sheet. Bake in a preheated 350°F oven for 6 to 8 minutes, until lightly golden. Cool completely before using.

If you have raw chicken breasts in the fridge and want to cook them for this salad, spray an 8-inch square glass baking dish with vegetable oil. Add the 2 (8-ounce) boneless, skinless chicken breasts in a single layer and drizzle on both sides with olive oil. Season with salt and pepper. Roast for 20 minutes, until cooked through. Cool for 10 minutes.

bruschettas, sandwiches & pizzas

Toasted Ciabatta with Shrimp, Tarragon, and Arugula

Bruschetta with Lamb, Fontina, and Greens

Mini Meatball Sandwiches

Grilled Pork and Fontina Sandwiches

Grilled Cheese with Spinach and Pancetta

Ham, Gruyère, and Apple Panini

Mediterranean Halibut Sandwiches

Arugula Pesto, Ricotta, and Smoked Mozzarella Pizza

Caramelized Onion, Sausage, and Basil Pizza

Chicken and Arugula
Pita Pockets

Antipasto Calzone

Burgers à la Pizzaiola

toasted ciabatta with shrimp, tarragon, and arugula

When two of my friends enrolled in an Italian language class, I decided to immerse them in the culture by cooking an Italian meal for them. I originally served this as a bruschetta, but later changed the recipe to a foot-long pizza with a ciabatta bread base so that it's faster and easier for a weeknight meal. (If you can't find ciabatta bread, look for any long, crusty-on-the-outside and airy-on-the-inside loaf.) Tarragon goes so well with shrimp and really elevates the flavors overall.

serves 4 to 6

bread

1 (1-pound) loaf ciabatta
   bread, trimmed and halved
   horizontally
Olive oil, for drizzling
1 garlic clove, halved

shrimp

3 tablespoons olive oil
1 large or 2 small shallots, thinly
   sliced
1 garlic clove, chopped
1 pound extra-large peeled and
   deveined shrimp
Kosher salt and freshly ground
   black pepper
6 plum tomatoes, chopped

¼ cup dry white wine
¼ cup low-sodium chicken
   broth
3 tablespoons chopped fresh
   tarragon leaves
2 packed cups (2 ounces)
   arugula, chopped
½ cup (4 ounces) mascarpone
   cheese, at room temperature

for the bread: Place an oven rack in the center of the oven. Preheat the oven to 400°F.

Arrange the bread halves on a baking sheet and drizzle with some olive oil. Bake until light golden, 13 to 15 minutes. Cool for 2 minutes. Rub the warm bread with the cut side of the garlic.

for the topping: While the bread is baking, in a large skillet, heat the oil over medium-high heat. Add the shallot and garlic and cook, stirring frequently, until soft, about 2 minutes. Season the shrimp with salt and pepper and add to the skillet. Cook for 3 to 4 minutes, until just pink and cooked through. Remove the shrimp to a cutting board.

In the same skillet, add the tomatoes and season with salt and pepper. Cook over medium-high heat until the tomatoes start to soften, about 4 minutes.

Meanwhile, cut the shrimp into ½-inch pieces.

recipe continues

Turn the heat under the skillet to high. Add the wine and, using a wooden spoon, scrape up the browned bits that cling to the bottom of the pan. Boil for 2 minutes. Add the broth and boil until most of the liquid has evaporated, about 2 minutes.

Remove the pan from the heat. Add the shrimp, tarragon, arugula, and mascarpone and stir until the mixture is creamy. Season to taste with salt and pepper. Spoon the creamy shrimp and sauce over the bread and sprinkle with salt and pepper. Cut into slices and serve.

bruschetta with lamb, fontina, and greens

My daughter, Jade, absolutely loves lamb. She prefers lamb chops so she can hold each one like a lollipop while she eats it. But I figured I'd come up with another way for her to enjoy the lamb that would also integrate her other favorite foods, like bread and cheese, along with some leafy greens to round everything out. Once the cheese is melted and gooey, neither Jade nor Todd or I can resist.

serves 4 to 6

bread

1 (1-pound) loaf ciabatta bread, trimmed and cut into 14 (½-inch-thick) slices
Olive oil, for drizzling
1 garlic clove, halved

lamb

3 tablespoons olive oil
1 pound ground lamb (see Cook's Note)
Kosher salt and freshly ground black pepper
4 garlic cloves, minced
1 teaspoon crushed red pepper flakes
5 packed cups (5 ounces) baby spinach
3 cups (12 ounces) shredded fontina cheese

for the bread: Place an oven rack in the center of the oven. Preheat the oven to 400°F.

Line a baking sheet with parchment. Arrange the bread slices in a single layer on the baking sheet and drizzle with olive oil. Bake until light golden, about 10 minutes. Cool for 2 minutes. Rub the warm toasts with the cut side of the garlic.

for the lamb: In a large skillet, heat the oil over medium-high heat. Add the lamb and season with 1 tablespoon salt and 1 teaspoon pepper. Cook, stirring frequently, until browned and cooked through, about 8 minutes. Add the minced garlic and red pepper flakes and cook until the garlic is fragrant, about 30 seconds. Add the spinach and cook until wilted, about 2 minutes. Season to taste with salt and pepper.

Spoon the lamb mixture on top of the toasts and arrange on the baking sheet. Sprinkle with the cheese and bake for 5 to 8 minutes, until the cheese is melted and bubbling. Cool for 2 minutes before serving.

cook's note

To mix things up a bit, you can substitute 1 pound spicy pork or turkey sausage, removed from the casings, for the lamb. Omit the red pepper flakes.

mini meatball sandwiches

The secret to these meatballs is the crushed corn flakes, which keep the meatballs light while adding a nice texture. Jade loves these, but so do Todd and I. Make a double batch of the meatballs and you can save the extras to top pasta later in the week.

makes 12 mini sandwiches; serves 4

¼ cup finely crushed corn flakes
1 tablespoon chopped fresh flat-leaf parsley leaves
1 large egg, lightly beaten
½ tablespoon olive oil
2 tablespoons ketchup, plus more for serving

2 tablespoons grated pecorino romano cheese
¼ teaspoon kosher salt
¼ teaspoon freshly ground black pepper

8 ounces (96% lean) ground beef
12 (2½-inch) sweet dinner rolls, such as King's Hawaiian, halved

Place an oven rack in the center of the oven. Preheat the oven to 375°F. Line a baking sheet with parchment.

In a medium bowl, stir together the corn flakes, parsley, egg, oil, 2 tablespoons ketchup, the romano cheese, salt, and pepper. Add the ground beef and gently stir to combine. With damp hands, roll the mixture into 12 mini meatballs. Place the meatballs on the prepared baking sheet, spacing them evenly. Bake for 20 minutes, until cooked through. Cool for 10 minutes.

Make an indentation in the center of the bottom halves of the rolls. Slice the meatballs in half and place two halves in each indentation. Add about 1 teaspoon of ketchup to each one and place the top half of the roll on top.

Arrange the sandwiches on a platter and serve.

grilled pork and fontina sandwiches

Sandwiches have a lunchtime-only reputation, but a sandwich as delicious and filling as this one definitely qualifies as dinner fare. The herbes de Provence create an amazing crust on the outside of the pork chops, which get nestled with cheese and lettuce between slices of sourdough bread. I like to serve these with Red Potato and Tomato Salad (page 200).

serves 4

2 (1-inch-thick) boneless pork loin chops (about 8 ounces each)
Olive oil, for drizzling
Kosher salt and freshly ground black pepper

2 teaspoons herbes de Provence
1 cup mayonnaise
½ packed cup chopped fresh basil leaves
Grated zest of 1 large lemon
2 teaspoons lemon juice

8 (½-inch-thick) slices country-style sourdough bread
4 romaine lettuce leaves, halved lengthwise
4 ounces fontina cheese, cut into 8 slices

Heat a grill pan over medium-high heat or heat a gas or charcoal grill.

Drizzle the pork chops on both sides with olive oil and season with ½ teaspoon salt and ¼ teaspoon pepper. Sprinkle both sides with the herbes de Provence. Grill for 10 minutes. Turn the chops over and cook for another 10 minutes, until cooked through; a meat thermometer inserted into the thickest part of the meat should register 165°F. Let the chops rest for 10 minutes.

While the chops are resting, in a small bowl, combine the mayonnaise, basil, lemon zest, lemon juice, 1¼ teaspoons salt, and ½ teaspoon pepper until smooth.

Cut the pork chops into 6 slices each. Spread one side of each slice of bread with some of the mayonnaise. Place lettuce leaves on top of 4 of the slices of bread. Arrange the cheese over the lettuce and top with the pork. Place the remaining 4 slices of bread on top and serve.

grilled cheese with spinach and pancetta

This is my Italian spin on a grilled cheese sandwich. I puree spinach with two kinds of cheese and some butter to make a creamy spread that I layer with crispy, salty pancetta.

serves 8

Vegetable oil cooking spray
6 ounces pancetta, sliced
⅛ inch thick
4 tablespoons (½ stick) unsalted butter, at room temperature
2 cups (8 ounces) shredded Monterey Jack cheese

2 cups (8 ounces) shredded mild Cheddar cheese
1 teaspoon kosher salt
1 tablespoon vegetable or canola oil

2 packed cups (2 ounces) coarsely chopped baby spinach
16 (⅓-inch-thick) slices country-style white or whole wheat bread

Place an oven rack in the center of the oven. Preheat the oven to 400°F.

Spray two baking sheets with vegetable oil. Lay the pancetta in a single layer on the baking sheets and bake for 12 to 14 minutes, until crispy and brown. Drain on paper towels. Cool for 5 minutes and then crumble.

In a food processor, combine the butter, both cheeses, the salt, oil, and 2 tablespoons water. Blend until smooth, adding a little more water, as needed, until the mixture is spreadable. Add the spinach and pulse until just combined.

Preheat a panini press (see Cook's Note).

Spread the cheese mixture over 8 of the slices of bread. Top with the crumbled pancetta and place the remaining bread slices on top. Grill the sandwiches, 2 at a time, until golden and crispy, 3 to 4 minutes. Cool for 2 minutes.

Cut each sandwich in half and arrange on a platter.

cook's note

If you don't have a panini press or indoor grill, use a grill pan. Preheat it before adding the sandwiches, weighting them down on top with a heavy pan, such as a cast-iron skillet. Be sure to flip the sandwiches halfway through cooking to brown the second side of them.

ham, gruyère, and apple panini

Ham and cheese never tasted so good, I promise. I add sautéed Granny Smith apples to give these panini a hint of sweet and tart and chopped fresh thyme for a savory and earthy essence of winter. These are great on their own but also pair nicely with Creamy Sweet Potato and Rosemary Soup (page 25).

serves 4

2 tablespoons unsalted butter, at room temperature
2 Granny Smith apples, peeled, cored, and sliced ¼ inch thick

1 tablespoon chopped fresh thyme leaves
8 (½-inch-thick) slices country-style white bread
½ cup whole-grain mustard

2 cups (8 ounces) shredded Gruyère cheese
8 (1-ounce) slices Black Forest ham

In a 12-inch skillet, melt the butter over medium heat. Add the apple slices and thyme. Cook, stirring occasionally, until the apples are slightly soft, about 4 minutes. Cool for 5 minutes.

Preheat a panini press (see Cook's Note).

Spread each bread slice with 1 tablespoon mustard. Arrange ¼ cup of cheese on each of 4 of the bread slices and top each with 2 slices of ham. Divide the apple mixture evenly over the ham. Add the remaining cheese and place the remaining 4 bread slices, mustard side down, on top. Grill until the cheese has melted and the tops are golden and crispy, 5 to 6 minutes.

cook's note

If you don't have a panini press or indoor grill, use a grill pan. Preheat it before adding the sandwiches, weighting them down on top with a heavy pan, such as a cast-iron skillet. Be sure to flip the sandwiches halfway through cooking to brown the second side of them.

mediterranean halibut sandwiches

Growing up in Italy, I spent many days on the beaches of the Mediterranean. This sandwich combines some of the area's best ingredients and flavors, including fresh fish, sun-dried tomatoes, basil, parsley, capers, and arugula. I love to pack up the sandwiches and bring them down to the beach near my home, where Todd, Jade, and I can have a dinner picnic.

serves 4

Vegetable oil cooking spray
2 (6-ounce) halibut fillets, skinned
Kosher salt and freshly ground black pepper
Olive oil, for drizzling
1 loaf of ciabatta bread, ends trimmed, halved lengthwise

1 garlic clove, halved
⅓ cup mayonnaise
¼ cup chopped sun-dried tomatoes
¼ cup chopped fresh basil leaves

2 tablespoons chopped fresh flat-leaf parsley leaves
1 tablespoon capers, drained and mashed
Grated zest of 1 large lemon
2 packed cups (2 ounces) arugula

Place an oven rack in the center of the oven. Preheat the oven to 450°F.

Spray a small baking sheet or glass baking dish with vegetable oil. Season the halibut on both sides with ½ teaspoon salt and ¼ teaspoon pepper. Place on the baking sheet and drizzle with olive oil. Bake for 10 to 15 minutes, until the fish is cooked through and the flesh flakes easily when poked with a fork. Set aside to cool completely, about 20 minutes.

Remove some of the dough from the top half of the bread. Brush the cut sides of the bread with olive oil. Put the bread on a baking sheet and bake in the oven for 6 to 8 minutes, until light golden. Remove and rub the cooked surface with the cut side of the garlic.

In a medium bowl, combine the mayonnaise, sun-dried tomatoes, basil, parsley, capers, lemon zest, ½ teaspoon salt, and ¼ teaspoon pepper.

Using a fork, flake the cooked fish and add to the mayonnaise mixture. Mix until incorporated. Spoon the filling on the bottom half of the bread. Top with the arugula. Add the top half of the bread and cut into 4 sandwiches.

arugula pesto, ricotta, and smoked mozzarella pizza

Creamy ricotta cheese is the base for all the delicious flavors here, most notably smoked mozzarella, which really gives the pizza a pronounced taste and aroma. Arugula makes the ricotta mixture a nice green hue, and the sliced red tomatoes help make this pizza as beautiful as it is yummy. This is total comfort food.

serves 4 to 6

Cornmeal, for dusting
½ cup whole-milk ricotta cheese
2 garlic cloves, crushed
1 teaspoon kosher salt
¼ teaspoon freshly ground
    black pepper

2 cups (8 ounces) shredded
    smoked mozzarella cheese
1 packed cup (1 ounce) arugula
Flour, for dusting

1 (1-pound) ball store-bought
    pizza dough
Olive oil, for drizzling
2 plum tomatoes, sliced ¼ inch
    thick

Place an oven rack in the center of the oven. Preheat the oven to 475°F. Sprinkle a heavy baking sheet (without sides) with cornmeal.

In a food processor, blend the ricotta, garlic, salt, and pepper until smooth. Add the smoked mozzarella and arugula. Pulse until just combined but still chunky.

On a lightly floured work surface, roll out the dough into a 14-inch circle, ¼ to ⅛ inch thick. Transfer the dough to the prepared baking sheet and drizzle with olive oil. Spread the ricotta mixture on top, leaving a 1-inch border. Arrange the tomato slices on top and drizzle with olive oil.

Bake for 15 to 16 minutes, until the crust is golden. Cut into wedges and serve.

caramelized onion, sausage, and basil pizza

I hosted a pizza party recently, and this is one of the pizzas I made for my friends to nibble on while they made their own creations. You can certainly make your own pizza dough, but for a quick weeknight meal by all means go for store-bought. Just make sure to let the dough warm up a bit at room temperature so that the gluten in the flour is relaxed enough to roll out. The sprinkle of cornmeal gives the crust an authentic texture.

serves 4 to 6

Vegetable oil cooking spray
Cornmeal, for dusting
2 medium sweet onions (about 1½ pounds), such as Maui or Walla Walla, thinly sliced
Olive oil
1 teaspoon balsamic vinegar

Kosher salt and freshly ground black pepper
Flour, for dusting
1 (1-pound) ball store-bought pizza dough
1 pound spicy turkey or pork sausage, casings removed, crumbled

¾ cup (about 3 ounces) crumbled gorgonzola or blue cheese
¼ cup chopped fresh basil leaves

Place an oven rack in the center of the oven and another rack in the upper third of the oven. Preheat the oven to 475°F. Spray a heavy baking sheet with vegetable oil. Sprinkle another heavy baking sheet (without sides) with cornmeal.

In a large bowl, toss the onions with 3 tablespoons olive oil, the balsamic vinegar, ½ teaspoon salt, and ¼ teaspoon pepper until coated. Arrange in a single layer on the oiled baking sheet. Bake in the upper third of the oven for 25 minutes, until golden. Cool slightly.

On a lightly floured work surface, roll out the dough into a 13-inch circle, about ¼ inch thick. Transfer the dough to the baking sheet sprinkled with cornmeal. Using a pastry brush, lightly brush the dough with olive oil. Bake at the same time as the onions, in the center of the oven, for 10 to 12 minutes, until the crust is crisp and lightly browned.

Once the dough is in the oven, in a large skillet, heat 1 tablespoon olive oil over medium-high heat. Add the sausage and season with salt and pepper. Cook, using a wooden spoon to break up the sausage, until cooked through, about 8 minutes. Set aside to cool slightly.

Spread the onions evenly over the dough, leaving a 1-inch border. Sprinkle the sausage and cheese on top. Bake for 5 minutes, until the cheese starts to melt and turns golden.

Sprinkle the pizza with chopped basil. Cut into wedges and serve.

chicken and arugula pita pockets

When you're really in a rush to put dinner on the table, I highly recommend these yummy sandwiches—lemony chicken salad and a peppery arugula pesto tucked into the pocket of a whole wheat pita. They're portable, too— perfect for a meal on the go.

serves 2 to 4

2 whole wheat pitas, halved and opened
¼ cup mayonnaise
1 teaspoon grated lemon zest

½ cup Arugula Pesto (recipe follows)
2 store-bought rotisserie chicken breasts, cut into ¼-inch pieces (about 2 cups)

8 cherry tomatoes, quartered
1 packed cup (1 ounce) arugula

Preheat the oven to 300°F.

Arrange the pita halves on a baking sheet and bake for 5 to 7 minutes, until warmed through (see Cook's Note).

In a large bowl, combine the mayonnaise, lemon zest, and pesto. Stir in the diced chicken.

Fill each pita half with the chicken mixture. Top each with some tomatoes and ¼ cup arugula and serve.

cook's note

If you have a toaster oven, by all means use it to warm the pitas.

arugula pesto
makes 1 cup

2 packed cups (2 ounces)
    arugula
1 garlic clove, peeled and
    halved
½ cup extra-virgin olive oil

½ cup grated Parmesan cheese
½ teaspoon kosher salt
¼ teaspoon freshly ground
    black pepper

Blend the arugula and garlic in a food processor until finely
chopped. With the machine running, gradually add the oil and
process until well blended. Transfer to a large bowl and stir in
Parmesan cheese, salt, and pepper.

antipasto calzone

A calzone is like a pizza turnover whereby the dough completely encases the filling. For the inside of this calzone, I combine ingredients you would typically find in a traditional Italian antipasto platter served at the beginning of a meal: cured meats, cheeses, olives, and an assortment of vegetables cooked any number of ways, or even pickled. This calzone is big and family size so be prepared for the "oohs" and "ahhs" when you pull it out of the oven. I like to serve this with warm marinara sauce on the side.

serves 4 to 6

Cornmeal, for dusting
Flour, for dusting
1 (1-pound) ball of store-bought pizza dough
1 cup (4 ounces) shredded provolone cheese (see Cook's Note)
1 cup (4 ounces) shredded fontina cheese (see Cook's Note)

1 (4-ounce) salami, cut into ½-inch pieces
2 jarred roasted red bell peppers, drained and cut into 1-inch pieces (about 1 cup)

¼ cup kalamata olives, coarsely chopped
¼ cup olive oil, plus more for drizzling
1 large egg, beaten
Marinara sauce (optional)

Place an oven rack in the center of the oven. Preheat the oven to 450°F. Sprinkle a heavy baking sheet with cornmeal.

On a lightly floured work surface, roll out the dough into a 13-inch circle, about ¼ inch thick. Transfer the dough to the prepared baking sheet.

In a medium bowl, combine the cheeses, salami, peppers, olives, and olive oil. Spoon the mixture onto one half of the dough, leaving a 1-inch border. Using a pastry brush, lightly brush the edges of the dough with the beaten egg. Fold the unfilled side of the dough over the filling and, using the tines of a fork, press the edges of the dough together to seal. Drizzle with olive oil. Using a paring knife, cut a ½-inch-wide slit in the top layer of dough.

cook's note

If grating the provolone and fontina cheeses by hand using a box grater, place them in the freezer for 15 to 20 minutes beforehand so that they remain firm while grating.

Bake for 20 to 25 minutes, until golden brown. Cool for 5 minutes. Cut the calzone into slices and serve with marinara sauce, if you choose.

burgers à la pizzaiola

I've taken the quintessential American burger and made an Italian version of it by adding ingredients you'd typically find on a pizza. And that's how this burger got its name: *pizzaiola* refers not only to a female pizza maker but also to the tomato and herb sauce used on pizzas.

serves 6

burgers

3 garlic cloves, smashed and peeled
5 sun-dried tomatoes in oil, drained
⅓ packed cup fresh basil leaves
3 tablespoons grated Parmesan cheese
2 cups (about 8 ounces) shredded mozzarella cheese

1 tablespoon tomato paste
½ teaspoon crushed red pepper flakes
1¼ teaspoons kosher salt
½ teaspoon freshly ground black pepper
1½ pounds (85% lean) ground beef

spread

1 cup (8 ounces) mascarpone cheese, at room temperature
⅓ cup chopped basil leaves
¾ teaspoon kosher salt
¾ teaspoon freshly ground black pepper

12 (½-inch-thick) slices rustic sourdough bread or 6 (4-inch) squares focaccia bread, sliced in half horizontally
2 tablespoons olive oil

for the burgers: Heat a grill pan over medium-high heat or heat a gas or charcoal grill.

In a food processor, pulse together the garlic, sun-dried tomatoes, basil leaves, Parmesan, ¾ cup of the mozzarella, the tomato paste, red pepper flakes, salt, and black pepper until blended. Transfer the mixture to a large bowl. Add the beef, and using a wooden spoon or clean hands, mix until combined. Form the mixture into 6 patties, each about ½ inch thick.

Grill the burgers for 4 minutes. Flip the burgers and add the remaining 1¼ cups mozzarella to the tops of the burgers, about 3 tablespoons each. Continue to cook for another 4 minutes, until cooked through. Remove from the grill and allow to rest for 5 minutes.

for the spread: In a medium bowl, combine the mascarpone cheese, basil, salt, and pepper until smooth.

Brush the bread with the olive oil and grill until lightly toasted, about 1 minute. Spread one side of each bread slice with the mascarpone spread. Place the burgers on 6 slices of the grilled bread and top with the remaining bread slices, mascarpone side down.

pasta &
grains

pasta & grains

Farfalle Pasta Salad with Broccoli and Pearl Onions

Whole-Grain Spaghetti with Brussels Sprouts and Mushrooms

Whole Wheat Linguine with Basil, Bacon, and Shrimp

Risotto with Currants, Pine Nuts, and Feta Cheese

Pasta alla Formiana

Pastina with Peas and Carrots

Penne in Almond Sauce

Spicy Linguine with Clams and Mussels

Sweet Corn and Basil Lasagna

Wagon Wheel Pasta with Pancetta and Peas

Whole Wheat Penne with Browned Butter, Arugula, and Walnuts

Pirate Pasta

Orzo with Smoky Tomato Vinaigrette

Ricotta Cheese, Lentil, and Brown Rice Rolls

farfalle pasta salad with broccoli and pearl onions

My sister, Eloisa, absolutely loved a farro, broccoli, and cipollini onion dish my mom used to make when we were kids. I re-created the dish, making it a more weeknight-friendly meal by replacing the farro with faster-cooking farfalle pasta and the cipollini onions with peeled and easy-to-find frozen pearl onions. Now, Eloisa can make this after work for both herself and for her son, Julian. Even better, it's great hot or cold, as a salad.

serves 4 to 6

1 pound farfalle pasta
¾ cup extra-virgin olive oil
1 (12-ounce) bag of frozen pearl onions, thawed
Kosher salt and freshly ground black pepper
3 garlic cloves, minced

1 pound broccoli, cut into small florets
1 (15-ounce) can cannellini beans, rinsed and drained
½ cup grated pecorino romano cheese

Grated zest and juice of 2 large lemons
2 tablespoons honey
1 cup (about 1 ounce) chopped fresh chives

Bring a large pot of salted water to a boil over high heat. Add the pasta and cook, stirring occasionally, until tender but still firm to the bite, 8 to 10 minutes. Drain and place in a large serving bowl.

In a large saucepan or Dutch oven, heat ¼ cup of the oil over medium-high heat. Add the onions and season with ½ teaspoon salt and ¼ teaspoon pepper. Cook, stirring occasionally, until golden and tender, about 10 minutes.

Add the garlic and cook for 30 seconds, until aromatic. Add the broccoli and sauté for 1 minute. Add ⅓ cup water and scrape up the browned bits that cling to the bottom of the pan with a wooden spoon. Cover the pan and cook until the broccoli is tender, about 4 minutes. Add the beans and cook for 1 minute, until warmed through. Transfer the mixture to the serving bowl. Add the pecorino cheese and toss with the pasta until coated.

In a small bowl, whisk together the lemon juice, lemon zest, remaining ½ cup olive oil, honey, ½ teaspoon salt, and ¼ teaspoon pepper. Stir in the chives.

Pour the dressing over the pasta and toss well until coated. Season to taste with salt and pepper and serve.

whole-grain spaghetti with brussels sprouts and mushrooms

I like to make this for my vegetarian and nonvegetarian friends alike. Cheese-coated whole-grain spaghetti, Brussels sprouts, and meaty mushrooms in a cream sauce strike just the right balance between healthy and a little indulgent.

serves 4 to 6

- 1 pound whole-grain or whole wheat spaghetti
- 1 cup grated pecorino romano cheese
- ¼ cup olive oil
- 1 medium onion, chopped
- 1 pound mushrooms, such as cremini, button, or stemmed shiitake, cleaned and cut into thick slices
- Kosher salt and freshly ground black pepper
- 1 pound Brussels sprouts, trimmed, halved, and thinly sliced
- 3 garlic cloves, minced
- 1 cup (8 ounces) crème fraîche, at room temperature
- ½ cup vegetable or chicken broth
- Grated zest of 1 large lemon
- ½ cup fresh lemon juice (from 2 large lemons)
- 1 cup slivered almonds, toasted (see Cook's Note)

Bring a large pot of salted water to a boil over high heat. Add the pasta and cook until tender but still firm to the bite, stirring occasionally, 8 to 10 minutes. Drain and transfer to a large serving bowl. Toss with ½ cup of the cheese.

In a large skillet, heat the oil over medium-high heat. Add the onion and mushrooms, 1 teaspoon salt, and ½ teaspoon pepper. Cook, stirring occasionally, until the onion is soft and the mushrooms are golden, about 6 minutes. Add the Brussels sprouts and garlic. Cook for 6 to 8 minutes, until the sprouts are soft.

Add the crème fraîche, vegetable broth, lemon zest, and lemon juice. Bring to a simmer and stir until the mixture forms a creamy sauce, about 2 minutes. Season with 2 teaspoons salt and 1 teaspoon pepper.

Pour the sauce over the pasta, add the almonds, and toss until coated. Sprinkle with the remaining ½ cup cheese and serve.

cook's note

To toast the almonds, arrange in a single layer on a baking sheet. Bake in a preheated 350°F oven for 8 to 10 minutes, until lightly toasted. Cool completely before using.

whole wheat linguine with basil, bacon, and shrimp

Whole wheat pastas have become increasingly popular; they're far tastier now than when they were first introduced, and they come with an appealing health benefit. I made this dish for my husband, Todd, when I wanted to persuade him that whole wheat pasta can be delicious. Needless to say, with the shrimp and bacon in this recipe, he became a convert.

serves 4 to 6

1 pound whole wheat linguine pasta
1 pound thick-cut bacon, chopped into ½-inch pieces
4 garlic cloves, minced

1 (14.5-ounce) can diced tomatoes, with juice
1 cup heavy cream
¾ cup bottled clam juice
1 cup chopped fresh basil leaves

Kosher salt and freshly ground black pepper
1½ pounds large peeled and deveined shrimp

Bring a large pot of salted water to a boil over high heat. Add the pasta and cook until tender but still firm to the bite, stirring occasionally, 10 to 12 minutes. Drain and transfer to a large serving bowl.

While the pasta is cooking, put the bacon in a large skillet. Turn on the heat to medium high and cook, stirring frequently, until the bacon is brown and crispy, about 10 minutes. Using a slotted spoon, remove the bacon and set aside.

In the same skillet, add the garlic and cook until aromatic, about 30 seconds. Add the tomatoes with their juice, the cream, clam juice, ½ cup of the basil, 2 teaspoons salt, and ½ teaspoon pepper. Bring to a boil and scrape up the browned bits that cling to the bottom of the pan with a wooden spoon. Reduce the heat to medium and simmer for 10 minutes, until slightly thickened.

Add the shrimp and cook, stirring occasionally, until just pink throughout and cooked through, about 3 minutes. Add the bacon and simmer until warmed through, 1 to 2 minutes.

Pour the shrimp mixture over the cooked pasta and toss until coated. Season to taste with salt and pepper, and garnish with the remaining ½ cup basil.

risotto with currants, pine nuts, and feta cheese

If you're thinking that risotto is way too complicated to make for a weeknight meal, I'm here to convince you otherwise. If you have thirty minutes, then your only job really is to be a dutiful stirrer as you coax the starches out of the grains of rice to create a creamy risotto. The finished one-pot dish is speckled with gems of sweet currants, salty feta, and crunchy pine nuts.

serves 4

5 cups low-sodium chicken broth
2 tablespoons olive oil
3 tablespoons unsalted butter
2 large or 4 small shallots, chopped

Kosher salt and freshly ground black pepper
1½ cups Arborio rice
½ cup dry white wine, such as Pinot Grigio
⅓ cup dried currants or raisins

¼ cup pine nuts, toasted (see Cook's Note)
⅔ cup (4 ounces) crumbled feta cheese
3 tablespoons chopped fresh flat-leaf parsley leaves

Heat the broth in a small saucepan and keep warm over low heat.

In a large saucepan or Dutch oven, heat the oil and 2 tablespoons of the butter over medium heat. Add the shallots and season with ½ teaspoon salt and ¼ teaspoon pepper. Cook for 2 minutes, until softened. Add the rice and cook, stirring often, until toasted, about 3 minutes. Add the wine and simmer, stirring occasionally, until evaporated, about 2 minutes.

Add ½ cup of the hot broth and cook, stirring, until completely absorbed. Continue adding the remaining broth, ½ cup at a time, cooking and stirring until the rice is creamy and tender, about 20 minutes.

Turn off the heat and stir in the remaining tablespoon butter, the currants, pine nuts, feta cheese, and parsley. Season to taste with salt and pepper. Transfer to a bowl and serve.

cook's note

To toast the pine nuts, arrange in a single layer on a baking sheet. Bake in a preheated 350°F oven for 6 to 8 minutes, until lightly toasted. Cool completely before using.

pasta alla formiana

Pasta alla Formiana, from the town of Formia in the coastal Lazio region of Italy (southwest of Naples), is a dish my aunt Raffy and I had once. The recipe is a surprise—because it doesn't require that the pasta be boiled before baking. Yup, that's right, it goes into the oven raw! I know it sounds crazy but it works. As long as the pasta has a hot liquid to absorb over a period of time, it will soften—which is why I go for mezze penne, which are half penne, or other smaller pasta cuts to ensure they cook through. For the liquid, I opt for fresh as well as canned crushed tomatoes, and for flavor, lots of oregano.

serves 4 to 6

Vegetable oil cooking spray
1 (28-ounce) can crushed
   tomatoes, with juice
½ cup low-sodium chicken
   broth
1 garlic clove, coarsely chopped

2 cups (8 ounces) mezze penne
   or other small pasta
⅓ cup olive oil, plus more for
   drizzling
2 tablespoons dried oregano
2 teaspoons kosher salt

½ teaspoon freshly ground
   black pepper
5 very ripe, extra-large or
   beefsteak tomatoes, sliced
   into ¼ inch thick

Place an oven rack in the upper third of the oven. Preheat the oven to 450°F. Spray an 8-inch square glass baking dish with vegetable oil.

In a food processor, blend together the crushed tomatoes and their juice, the chicken broth, and garlic. Pour into a medium saucepan and bring to a boil over medium-high heat. Stir in the pasta, olive oil, oregano, salt, and pepper.

While the sauce is heating, line the bottom and sides of the baking dish with half to two-thirds of the tomato slices. Pour the pasta mixture into the pan and spread evenly. Arrange the remaining tomato slices in an overlapping layer on top of the pasta mixture, making sure the mixture is completely covered. Drizzle with a little olive oil.

Put the baking dish on a rimmed baking sheet and bake for 30 minutes, until the tomatoes are slightly crispy and the pasta is cooked. Cool for 5 minutes and serve.

pastina with peas and carrots

Every Italian child has eaten his or her fair share of pastina. My mom used to make this exact dish for me when I was growing up in Rome. It was my favorite. Now that I'm a mom, I often make it for Jade, and she loves it, too. The traditional pastina cut is little stars, which is so perfect for kids because they look like something fun to eat, but you can use any small shape.

serves 6

1 (16-ounce) box pastina or other small-shaped pasta, such as farfallini
¼ cup olive oil
1 large yellow onion, finely diced
4 medium carrots, peeled and cut into ½-inch pieces

2 cups low-sodium chicken broth
2 cups frozen petite peas, thawed
1 cup (8 ounces) cream cheese, at room temperature

1 cup (8 ounces) mascarpone cheese, at room temperature
Kosher salt and freshly ground black pepper
¼ cup chopped fresh basil leaves

Bring a large pot of salted water to a boil over high heat. Add the pasta and cook until tender but still firm to the bite, stirring occasionally, 7 to 9 minutes. Drain the pasta and transfer to a large serving bowl.

In a large nonstick skillet, heat the oil over medium heat. Add the onion and cook, stirring occasionally, until soft, about 7 minutes. Add the carrots and broth and bring to a boil. Reduce the heat so that the mixture simmers and cook for 5 minutes.

Add the peas to the pan and cook for 2 minutes, until the peas are warmed through and the carrots are tender. Remove the pan from the heat and add the cheeses, 2 teaspoons salt, and ½ teaspoon pepper. Stir until the mixture is incorporated and forms a sauce.

Pour the sauce over the pasta and season to taste with salt and pepper. Garnish with chopped basil and serve.

cook's note

To make this a more substantial dish, consider adding a store-bought rotisserie chicken breast, shredded.

penne in almond sauce

Almond and walnut sauces, or pestos, are very common in Italian cooking not only because the ingredients are so readily available but also because pestos are easy to make while packing a lot of flavor. I use blanched almonds so that the color and the texture of the sauce is more appealing and smooth. Don't worry, the sauce will seem very loose but it will quickly thicken as you add the cheese.

serves 4 to 6

1 pound penne pasta
2 cups (9 ounces) blanched, slivered almonds
3 cups low-sodium chicken broth
¼ cup olive oil
3 garlic cloves, peeled and smashed

2 store-bought rotisserie chicken breasts, skinned and cut into ½-inch cubes (about 2 cups)
1 cup frozen petite peas
1 cup heavy cream

Grated zest of 1 large lemon
Kosher salt and freshly ground black pepper
2 cups grated Parmesan cheese
½ cup chopped fresh basil leaves

Bring a large pot of salted water to a boil over high heat. Add the pasta and cook until tender but still firm to the bite, stirring occasionally, 8 to 10 minutes. Drain and reserve about 1 cup of the pasta water. Transfer the cooked pasta to a serving bowl.

In a blender, combine the almonds, chicken broth, olive oil, and garlic. Blend until the mixture is smooth. Pour the mixture into a large skillet and turn the heat on to medium. Bring the mixture to a boil and cook, stirring constantly, until the mixture thickens slightly, about 2 minutes. Add the chicken, peas, cream, and lemon zest. Cook, stirring frequently, until the chicken is heated through, about 4 minutes (mixture will be thick). Season with 1 tablespoon salt and 1½ teaspoons pepper.

Add ½ cup of the Parmesan cheese to the pasta and toss until the pasta is coated. Add the chicken mixture, the remaining 1½ cups cheese, and the basil. Toss the ingredients together, adding the reserved pasta water, as needed, to loosen the sauce. Season to taste with salt and pepper, and serve.

cook's note

To reheat, add a little cream or broth to the mixture to loosen up the pasta.

spicy linguine with clams and mussels

If you love shellfish, you'll go for this classic dish inspired by the many versions I've eaten while visiting the Italian island of Capri. Mussels and clams are readily available at the seafood counter of most supermarkets as well as at any fish store, and, contrary to the belief of many, they're rather inexpensive. To clean clams and mussels, I submerge them in a bowl of water doused with coarse cornmeal, which forces them to expel any sand. Give the shells a quick scrub with a brush and remove any beards: minimal prep for a dish that cooks up quickly and tastes fantastic.

serves 4 to 6

1 pound linguine pasta
2 tablespoons unsalted butter, at room temperature
¼ cup chopped fresh flat-leaf parsley leaves
Kosher salt and freshly ground black pepper

3 tablespoons olive oil
2 large or 4 small shallots, minced
3 garlic cloves, minced
1 cup dry white wine, such as Pinot Grigio

1 cup vegetable broth
½ teaspoon crushed red pepper flakes
12 littleneck clams, cleaned
12 mussels, cleaned

Bring a large pot of salted water to a boil over high heat. Add the pasta and cook until tender but still firm to the bite, stirring occasionally, 8 to 10 minutes. Drain and transfer to a large serving bowl. Add the butter and parsley and toss until coated. Season with ½ teaspoon salt and ¼ teaspoon pepper.

Meanwhile, in a large skillet or saucepan, heat the oil over medium-high heat. Add the shallots and season with salt and pepper. Cook, stirring frequently, until soft, 3 to 4 minutes. Add the garlic and cook for 30 seconds, until aromatic. Add the wine and simmer for 2 minutes, until the liquid has reduced by half.

Add the broth, red pepper flakes, clams, and mussels. Bring the mixture to a simmer. Cover the pan with a tight-fitting lid and cook until all the shellfish have opened, 5 to 8 minutes.

Using tongs, remove the shellfish from the pan and reserve. (Discard any unopened shellfish.) Season the cooking liquid with 2 teaspoons salt and 1 teaspoon pepper. Pour the shellfish cooking liquid over the pasta and toss well. Season to taste with additional salt and pepper, if needed. Arrange the reserved shellfish on top of the pasta and serve.

sweet corn and basil lasagna

No-boil noodles and a food processor are what make this lasagna a weeknight-dinner friend. Both help to put a super-creamy, provolone-cheesy, comforting, and downright amazing pasta dish on the table for the family. One tip to minimize clean-up and avoid hand-grating the cheese: use the shredding attachment of the food processor to grate the provolone first. Then, without having to wash the bowl, you can switch to the blade to make the sweet corn and basil filling. Smiles all around!

serves 4 to 6

Vegetable oil cooking spray
3 cups frozen corn, thawed
½ cup heavy cream, at room temperature
2 garlic cloves, peeled
1 cup (8 ounces) mascarpone cheese, at room temperature

1½ cups grated pecorino romano cheese
Grated zest of 1 large lemon
¼ teaspoon kosher salt
¼ teaspoon freshly ground black pepper
¾ packed cup chopped fresh basil leaves

1½ cups (6 ounces) shredded sharp provolone cheese (see Cook's Note, page 72)
6 no-boil lasagna sheets (about half a 9-ounce box)
Olive oil, for drizzling

Place an oven rack in the center of the oven. Preheat the oven to 375°F. Spray an 8-inch square glass baking dish with vegetable oil cooking spray.

In a food processor, blend the corn, cream, and garlic until chunky. Add the mascarpone cheese, 1 cup of the romano cheese, the lemon zest, salt, and pepper. Blend until smooth. Add the basil and pulse until just combined.

Spread one-third of the corn mixture on the bottom of the prepared baking dish. Sprinkle with one-third of the provolone cheese. Place 2 lasagna sheets on top. Repeat twice with the remaining corn mixture, provolone cheese, and lasagna sheets. Sprinkle with the remaining ½ cup romano cheese and drizzle with olive oil.

Bake for 25 to 30 minutes, until the top is golden brown and the filling is bubbling. Cool for 10 minutes. Cut into 6 pieces and serve.

wagon wheel pasta with pancetta and peas

When making pasta dishes for kids, I try to choose a cut that will be fun to eat, like these wagon wheels. Then I throw in a bunch of veggies, such as the snap peas, edamame, and green peas here along with a little protein—in this case, crispy rendered pancetta. Then dinner is served. Happy kids, and happy parents, with full bellies.

serves 4 to 6

1 pound wagon wheel–shaped pasta (rotelle)
¼ cup plus 1 tablespoon extra-virgin olive oil
8 ounces pancetta, finely diced (about 2¼ cups)
2 large or 4 small shallots, chopped

½ cup low-sodium chicken broth
1½ cups (5 ounces) sugar snap peas, cut into 1-inch pieces
1½ cups (9 ounces) shelled edamame beans
1 cup frozen petite peas, thawed

1 cup grated Parmesan cheese
1 teaspoon kosher salt
¼ teaspoon freshly ground black pepper
¼ cup chopped fresh mint leaves

Bring a large pot of salted water to a boil over high heat. Add the pasta and cook until tender but still firm to the bite, stirring occasionally, 8 to 10 minutes. Drain and reserve about 1 cup of the pasta water.

In a large skillet, heat 1 tablespoon of the oil over medium-high heat. Add the pancetta and cook, stirring frequently, until golden and crisp, 6 to 8 minutes. Using a slotted spoon, remove the pancetta and drain on a paper towel–lined plate.

Add the shallots to the pan and cook until soft, 2 to 3 minutes. Add the broth and scrape up the browned bits that cling to the bottom of the pan with a wooden spoon. Stir in the snap peas and simmer for 2 minutes, until tender.

Add the pasta, cooked pancetta, edamame, petite peas, Parmesan cheese, the remaining ¼ cup olive oil, the salt, pepper, and mint. Toss until coated, adding the reserved pasta water, 1 tablespoon at a time, as needed to loosen the sauce. Transfer to a bowl and serve.

whole wheat penne with browned butter, arugula, and walnuts

I absolutely love the nutty, amazing smell and flavor of browned butter. It brings out the best in whole wheat pasta and makes a natural pairing with walnuts. Grape tomatoes and arugula add freshness while Parmesan cheese and capers deliver a punch of salty flavor.

serves 4 to 6

¼ cup extra-virgin olive oil
Grated zest and juice of 1 large lemon
Kosher salt and freshly ground black pepper
1 pound whole wheat or multigrain penne rigate pasta

4 tablespoons (½ stick) unsalted butter, cut into ½-inch pieces, at room temperature
4 packed cups (4 ounces) baby arugula
1 cup cherry or grape tomatoes, halved

1 cup grated Parmesan cheese
¾ cup chopped walnuts, toasted (see Cook's Note)
2 tablespoons capers, rinsed and drained

In a small bowl, whisk together the olive oil, lemon zest, lemon juice, 2 teaspoons salt, and ½ teaspoon pepper until smooth.

Bring a large pot of salted water to a boil over high heat. Add the pasta and cook until tender but still firm to the bite, stirring occasionally, 8 to 10 minutes. Drain and reserve about 1 cup of the pasta water.

Meanwhile, in a high-sided skillet, heat the butter over medium heat until melted. Simmer until the butter is foamy. Continue to cook until the butter has a nutty aroma and turns a caramel color, 3 to 5 minutes.

Remove the pan from the heat. Add the pasta, dressing, arugula, tomatoes, Parmesan cheese, walnuts, and capers. Toss until coated, adding the reserved pasta water, 1 tablespoon at a time, to loosen the sauce, if needed. Season to taste with salt and pepper. Transfer to a large bowl and serve.

cook's note

To toast the walnuts, arrange in a single layer on a baking sheet. Bake in a preheated 350°F oven for 6 to 8 minutes, until lightly toasted. Cool completely before using.

pirate pasta

I call this "pirate" pasta because the dish is full of little treasures: mushrooms, tuna, olives, and capers. Each bite contains a gem, whether it's the briny crunch of the caper or the earthy and meaty texture of the mushrooms and olives. I particularly love the addition of the tuna, as it's a pleasant reminder of the pasta and tuna dishes that are so common in Italy.

serves 4 to 6

1 pound penne pasta
1½ cups grated pecorino romano cheese
¼ cup olive oil
8 ounces mushrooms, such as cremini, button, or stemmed shiitake, sliced
2 garlic cloves, peeled

Kosher salt and freshly ground black pepper
1 (10-ounce) or 2 (5-ounce) cans tuna in olive oil, such as Tonnino, drained
½ cup (about 18) medium green olives, pitted and halved
¼ cup tomato paste

2 tablespoons capers, rinsed and drained
½ teaspoon crushed red pepper flakes
½ cup low-sodium chicken broth
½ cup chopped fresh basil leaves

Bring a large pot of salted water to a boil over high heat. Add the pasta and cook until tender but still firm to the bite, stirring occasionally, 8 to 10 minutes. Drain and reserve about 1 cup of the pasta water. Transfer the pasta and 1 cup of the cheese to a large bowl and toss until coated.

In a medium skillet, heat the olive oil over medium-high heat. Add the mushrooms, garlic, ½ teaspoon salt, and ¼ teaspoon pepper. Cook, stirring frequently, for 5 to 6 minutes, until the mushrooms begin to brown. Add the tuna, olives, tomato paste, capers, red pepper flakes, 1½ teaspoons salt, and ¼ teaspoon pepper. Using a wooden spoon, break up the tuna into 1-inch pieces. Add the chicken broth and bring the mixture to a boil. Remove the garlic and discard.

Pour the tuna mixture over the pasta; add the remaining ½ cup cheese and the basil. Toss until coated, using the reserved pasta water, 1 tablespoon at a time, to loosen the sauce as needed. Season to taste with salt and pepper, and serve.

orzo with smoky tomato vinaigrette

I've been on a "smoky" kick lately, exploring ways to integrate this distinct flavor into new recipes, such as by using smoked paprika or by charring on the grill. In this case, I char the cherry tomatoes in a skillet and add some smoked salt, which you can find in a well-stocked grocery store, to make the smoky dressing for the orzo. Tart cider vinegar and naturally sweet honey temper the smokiness and help round out the sauce. I like this as is— as a terrific vegetarian main course—but Todd loves it when I add some ground beef to the mix.

serves 4 to 6

1 pound (2 pints) cherry
   tomatoes
Kosher salt
1 pound orzo pasta
½ cup packed fresh basil leaves,
   torn

2 tablespoons apple cider
   vinegar
2 tablespoons extra-virgin
   olive oil
1 tablespoon honey

Smoked salt
Freshly ground black pepper
⅓ cup grated Parmesan cheese

Place the tomatoes in a large nonstick skillet over medium-high heat. Cook, shaking the pan occasionally, until the tomatoes are tender and the skins are charred in spots, about 10 minutes. Set aside to cool.

Bring a large pot of salted water to a boil over high heat. Add the pasta and cook until tender but still firm to the bite, stirring occasionally, 8 to 10 minutes. Drain and transfer to a large serving bowl.

Combine the tomatoes, basil, vinegar, olive oil, honey, 1 tablespoon smoked salt, and ¼ teaspoon pepper in a blender. Blend until smooth.

Pour the tomato vinaigrette over the pasta and toss until coated. Sprinkle with the Parmesan cheese. Season to taste with smoked salt and pepper, and serve.

ricotta cheese, lentil, and brown rice rolls

Inspired by a dish my friend Hannah made for me, this easy recipe takes advantage of canned lentils and pre-cooked brown rice, widely available in stores these days. I mix them with ricotta to make a filling for blanched Swiss chard leaves. It's a vegetarian dish that even meat-eaters will love.

serves 4 to 6

Butter for the baking dish
5 large Swiss chard leaves (about 14 ounces)
1 (15-ounce) can of cooked lentils, rinsed and drained
1½ cups store-bought ready-cooked brown rice
¼ cup (4 ounces) whole-milk ricotta cheese, at room temperature

1 cup grated Parmesan cheese
⅓ cup plus 2 tablespoons olive oil
1 packed cup (1 ounce) baby arugula leaves, chopped
½ cup chopped fresh mint leaves

2 garlic cloves, minced
¾ teaspoon kosher salt
½ teaspoon freshly ground black pepper
1 (26-ounce) jar of marinara or tomato-basil sauce

Place an oven rack in the center of the oven. Preheat the oven to 400°F. Butter an 8 x 8-inch glass baking dish and place it on a rimmed baking sheet. Set aside.

Bring a large pot of salted water to a boil over high heat. Remove the thick stem from the center of each chard leaf. Cut each leaf in half lengthwise. Trim the ends to make each leaf-half about 7 inches long and 4 inches wide. Add the leaves to the boiling water and cook for 10 seconds. Remove the leaves and rinse with cold water. Drain on paper towels.

In a medium bowl, mix the lentils, brown rice, ricotta cheese, ½ cup of the Parmesan cheese, ⅓ cup of the olive oil, the arugula, mint, garlic, salt, and pepper.

Spoon 1 cup of the marinara sauce on the bottom of the prepared pan. Spoon a heaping ⅓ cup of the filling onto the end of each leaf and roll up like a burrito, tucking in the sides as you go. Arrange the rolls, seam side down, in a single layer on top of the sauce. Spoon the remaining sauce on top and sprinkle with the remaining ½ cup Parmesan cheese. Drizzle with the remaining 2 tablespoons olive oil.

Slide the baking sheet into the oven and bake for 25 minutes, until the cheese begins to brown and the rolls are heated through. Cool for 5 minutes and serve.

meat, poultry & fish

meat, poultry & fish

Filet Mignon with Rosemary and Mushroom Gravy

Beef and Mushroom Skewers with Soy and Scallion Butter

Grilled Sirloin Steaks with Pepper and Caper Salsa

Rib-Eye Steaks with Smoky Arrabiata Sauce

Herbed Lamb Chops with Homemade BBQ Sauce

Roasted Pork with Smoky Red Pepper Sauce

Spiced Pork Chops with Sweet and Sour Glaze

Chicken with Tarragon and White Wine

Chicken Meunière with Tomato and Parsley Sauce

Crispy Chicken with Rosemary-Lemon Salt

Turkey and Pancetta Pot Pies

Salmon Cakes with Lemon-Caper Yogurt Sauce

Balsamic-Glazed Salmon

Broiled Tilapia with Mustard-Chive Sauce

Grilled Fish Kebobs with Parsley and Garlic Butter

filet mignon with rosemary and mushroom gravy

For special weeknight meals, I turn to filet mignon steaks. They're cut from the short ends of the tenderloin, the choicest cut of meat, which makes them a bit pricy. If you're not up for the splurge, try this recipe with a more economical cut, like a sirloin or flatiron. I sear the meat in a skillet first, and use the browned bits on the bottom of the pan for the mushroom gravy.

serves 4

Vegetable oil cooking spray
5 tablespoons olive oil
2 (8-ounce) filet mignon steaks
Kosher salt and freshly ground
  black pepper
2 large or 4 small shallots,
  minced

2 cups (about 5 ounces)
  coarsely chopped assorted
  mushrooms, such as
  cremini, button, and
  stemmed shiitake
½ cup dry Marsala wine
1½ cups low-sodium beef broth

1½ tablespoons chopped fresh
  rosemary leaves
1½ tablespoons all-purpose
  flour
3 tablespoons unsalted butter,
  at room temperature

Place an oven rack in the center of the oven. Preheat the oven to 400°F. Spray a small baking sheet with vegetable oil.

In a large skillet, heat 3 tablespoons of the oil over medium-high heat. Season the steaks on all sides with 1 teaspoon salt and ½ teaspoon pepper. Add the steaks to the pan and brown on all sides, about 4 minutes. Transfer the steaks to the prepared baking sheet and roast for 10 minutes for medium-rare. Transfer to a cutting board and let them rest for 5 minutes.

Meanwhile, in the same skillet as used for the steak, heat the remaining 2 tablespoons oil over medium-high heat. Add the shallots and mushrooms and season with salt and pepper. Cook for 5 minutes, until the shallots are soft. Add the wine and scrape up the browned bits that cling to the bottom of the pan with a wooden spoon. Boil until most of the liquid has evaporated, about 2 minutes. Add the beef broth and rosemary. Using a whisk, whisk in the flour until smooth. Bring the mixture to a boil. Reduce the heat so that the mixture simmers and cook, stirring occasionally, until half of the liquid has evaporated and the sauce has thickened slightly, about 10 minutes. Remove the pan from the heat and stir in the butter until smooth. Season to taste with salt and pepper.

Cut the steaks across the grain into ¼-inch-thick slices and arrange on a platter. Pour the sauce into a serving bowl and serve alongside the meat.

beef and mushroom skewers with soy and scallion butter

Kebobs are a frequent dinner request in my home: Todd and Jade like eating them with their hands; I like the fact that they combine a meat and side into one easy recipe. The mushrooms and beef flavor each other while cooking, and the char from the grill makes these even tastier. Serve over rice or couscous and finish with a pat of savory soy and scallion butter.

serves 4 to 6

butter
8 tablespoons (1 stick) unsalted butter, at room temperature
3 small scallions, white and pale green parts only, finely chopped
1 garlic clove, minced
1½ tablespoons soy sauce

skewers
⅓ cup olive oil
4 garlic cloves, minced
1 teaspoon kosher salt
1 teaspoon freshly ground black pepper

1 (1¼-pound) sirloin steak, about ¾ inch thick, cut into 24 (1½-inch) pieces
24 (1-inch diameter) button or cremini mushrooms(about 12 ounces)

for the butter: In a small bowl, using a fork, combine the butter, scallions, garlic, and soy sauce until smooth.

for the skewers: In a small bowl, mix the olive oil, garlic, salt, and pepper. Alternating meat and mushrooms, thread 3 pieces of meat and 3 mushrooms onto each of 8 skewers (see Cook's Note). Arrange the skewers in a single layer on a baking sheet. Spoon the oil mixture over the top and marinate for 15 minutes.

Heat a grill pan over medium-high heat or preheat a gas or charcoal grill. Grill the skewers for 3 to 5 minutes on each side for medium. Transfer the skewers to a platter and let rest for 5 minutes.

Serve the skewers topped with the butter.

cook's note
I find long metal skewers easiest to use. If you're using wooden skewers, make sure to soak them in water for at least 15 minutes before using to prevent them from burning on the grill.

grilled sirloin steaks with pepper and caper salsa

Sirloin steaks are perfect for grilling. They're a tender, juicy cut of meat that requires quick, high-heat cooking, as opposed to a braise or a stew, to achieve a nice crust on both sides and the perfect doneness on the inside. This pepper and caper salsa tastes fantastic on top of the grilled steaks because of the sweetness and smokiness of the peppers, and the briny bites of capers.

serves 4 to 6

salsa
3 tablespoons extra-virgin olive oil
3 tablespoons balsamic vinegar
¼ cup capers, rinsed and drained
3 tablespoons chopped fresh flat-leaf parsley leaves
½ teaspoon kosher salt
¼ teaspoon freshly ground black pepper
1 (12-ounce) jar of roasted red bell peppers, drained and sliced ½ inch thick
1 (12-ounce) jar of roasted yellow bell peppers, drained and sliced ½ inch thick

steaks
4 (8-ounce) boneless sirloin steaks, about 1 inch thick
2 teaspoons smoked salt or kosher salt
2 teaspoons herbes de Provence
Olive oil, for drizzling

for the salsa: In a small bowl, whisk together the olive oil, balsamic vinegar, capers, parsley, salt, and pepper until smooth. Add the bell peppers and toss until coated.

for the steaks: Heat a grill pan over medium-high heat or preheat a gas or charcoal grill. Season the steaks on both sides with the smoked salt and herbes de Provence. Drizzle with olive oil and grill for 4 to 6 minutes on each side for medium-rare. Let the steaks rest for 5 minutes before serving.

To serve, thinly slice the steak and top with the salsa.

rib-eye steaks with smoky arrabiata sauce

Rib-eyes are tender, flavorful, and a perfect cut for grilling. Smoky arrabiata sauce adds another level of flavor from the aromatics, sugar, and smoked paprika and it elevates the steak from good to fantastic. Even better, the sauce makes about 3½ cups, so you can use 1 cup for the steaks and save the rest to serve as a sauce for a pound of pasta.

serves 4 to 6

1 (28-ounce) can crushed tomatoes
1 large onion, coarsely chopped
3 garlic cloves, crushed and peeled
2 tablespoons capers, drained and rinsed

1 (4-inch-long) serrano or 2 Thai chiles, stemmed, half of the seeds removed, coarsely chopped
2 tablespoons sugar
1 tablespoon smoked paprika, or more to taste

Kosher salt and freshly ground black pepper
2 (1-pound) rib-eye steaks, each about 1 inch thick
2 tablespoons olive oil

In a food processor, combine the tomatoes, onion, garlic, capers, chili, sugar, paprika, and 2 teaspoons salt. Process until slightly chunky. Pour the sauce into a medium saucepan and bring to a simmer over medium-low heat. Cook for 25 minutes, until thickened. Season to taste with additional salt and smoked paprika. (Once cool, the sauce will keep for up to 1 week in an airtight container in the refrigerator. Reheat before serving.)

Heat a grill pan over medium-high heat or preheat a gas or charcoal grill. Season the steaks on both sides with 2 teaspoons salt and 1 teaspoon pepper. Drizzle the steaks on both sides with the olive oil. Grill for 5 to 6 minutes on each side for medium-rare. Cover loosely with foil and let the steaks rest for 5 minutes.

Slice the steaks across the grain into ¼-inch-thick slices and pour 1 cup of the sauce on top.

herbed lamb chops with homemade bbq sauce

Jade absolutely loves lamb chops. To give the lamb chops an added dimension of flavor, I season them with herbes de Provence, a mixture of dried thyme, lavender, basil, fennel—a really nice combination. Dried herbs are more concentrated than fresh herbs, so you don't need a lot to make an impact. Serve with this homemade barbecue sauce for dipping, and you're guaranteed a happy table of eaters in very little time.

serves 4

barbecue sauce

1 (15-ounce) can of tomato sauce or tomato puree
1 small onion, peeled and quartered, root end left intact
1 garlic clove, peeled and smashed
½ cup apple cider vinegar
½ packed cup light brown sugar
⅓ cup tomato paste
1 tablespoon Worcestershire sauce
1 tablespoon balsamic vinegar
2 teaspoons kosher salt
1 cinnamon stick or a pinch of ground cinnamon

lamb chops

1 pound (about 8 or 9) baby lamb chops
1 tablespoon kosher salt
½ teaspoon freshly ground black pepper
2 tablespoons olive oil
1½ tablespoons herbes de Provence

for the barbecue sauce: Combine the tomato sauce, onion, garlic, apple cider vinegar, sugar, tomato paste, Worcestershire sauce, balsamic vinegar, salt, and cinnamon stick (or ground cinnamon, if using) in a medium saucepan. Bring the mixture to a simmer and cook, stirring occasionally, for 30 minutes, until thick. Cool for 30 minutes. Remove the onion, garlic, and cinnamon stick and discard. Refrigerate until ready to use (for up to 1 week).

for the lamb chops: Heat a grill pan over medium-high heat or preheat a gas or charcoal grill.

Season the chops on both sides with the salt and pepper. Drizzle with the oil and sprinkle the herbes de Provence on both sides. Grill for 2 to 3 minutes on each side, until medium rare. Let rest for 5 minutes before serving with the barbecue sauce.

roasted pork with smoky red pepper sauce

Pork tenderloin is a very moist cut of meat. But, as it's lean and boneless, it doesn't pack a ton of flavor. So I help it along by seasoning the meat well, then dressing it with a bell pepper sauce that uses smoked paprika to bring the dish to life.

serves 4 to 6

6 tablespoons olive oil
2 (1½-pound) pork tenderloins, halved crosswise
Kosher salt and freshly ground black pepper
1 small onion, diced
1 medium red bell pepper, cored, seeded, and diced into ½-inch pieces

1 medium yellow bell pepper, cored, seeded, and diced into ½-inch pieces
1 medium orange bell pepper, cored, seeded, and diced into ½-inch pieces
3 garlic cloves, minced
1¼ cups red wine, such as Syrah or Cabernet Sauvignon

2½ tablespoons smoked paprika
1 (10.75-ounce) can tomato puree
1 dried bay leaf
¼ cup chopped fresh flat-leaf parsley leaves

Place an oven rack in the center of the oven. Preheat the oven to 400°F.

In a large skillet, heat 2 tablespoons of the oil over high heat. Rub 1 tablespoon of the oil over the pork and season with 2 teaspoons salt and 1 teaspoon pepper. Add the pork to the pan and brown on all sides, about 8 minutes. Transfer the pork to a roasting pan and roast for 25 to 30 minutes, until a meat thermometer inserted into the thickest part of the pork registers 165°F. Transfer the pork to a cutting board to rest for 10 minutes.

Meanwhile, in the same skillet used for the pork, heat the remaining 3 tablespoons oil over medium-high heat. Add the onion, bell peppers, and garlic and cook, stirring frequently, for 8 to 10 minutes, until softened. Add the wine and cook for 2 minutes, scraping up the brown bits that cling to the bottom of the pan with a wooden spoon. Stir in the paprika, tomato puree, and bay leaf. Bring the mixture to a boil. Reduce the heat and simmer for 25 to 30 minutes, until the sauce thickens. Remove the bay leaf and transfer the mixture to a food processor or blender. Blend until smooth. Season to taste with salt and pepper.

Thinly slice the pork and arrange on a platter. Spoon the sauce on top. Garnish with chopped parsley and serve.

spiced pork chops
with sweet and sour glaze

These pork chops were my brother Igor's childhood favorite, especially with the sweet and sour glaze, which in Italian is called *agrodolce; agro* means "sour" and *dolce* means "sweet." Admittedly, the crushed red pepper wasn't something that Igor would eat as a child because it was too spicy. But as he got older and developed a taste for spicy food, I thought it'd be appropriate to make him this grown-up version.

serves 4

¼ cup olive oil, plus more as needed
4 (8-ounce) boneless pork chops, about 1 inch thick
Kosher salt and freshly ground black pepper
1 teaspoon crushed red pepper flakes

½ cup balsamic vinegar
½ cup honey
2 garlic cloves, minced
3 scallions, white and pale green parts only, finely chopped

1 teaspoon chopped fresh rosemary leaves
½ stick (4 tablespoons) unsalted butter, cut into ½-inch cubes, at room temperature

In a large, heavy skillet, heat the olive oil over medium-high heat. Season the pork chops with 1 teaspoon salt, ½ teaspoon pepper, and the red pepper flakes. Add the pork to the pan and cook for 8 to 10 minutes on each side, until cooked through. Transfer the pork to a platter, cover loosely with foil, and let rest for 5 minutes.

Meanwhile, in a small saucepan, bring the vinegar, honey, garlic, scallions, and rosemary to a boil over medium-high heat. Stir occasionally until the honey has dissolved. Lower the heat and simmer for 8 to 10 minutes, until slightly reduced. Remove the pan from the heat and whisk in the butter until smooth. Season to taste with salt and pepper.

Drizzle the pork chops with the glaze and serve.

chicken with tarragon and white wine

Boneless chicken will cook faster and braising it will ensure the meat stays tender while the onion, tarragon, white wine, and mustard promise to create a super-tasty sauce. While the chicken cooks, prepare some rice, baked potatoes, pasta, or any other starch because you'll have plenty of sauce to go around.

serves 4

¼ cup vegetable oil
2 (8-ounce) boneless and
    skinless chicken breasts
4 (4-ounce) boneless and
    skinless chicken thighs
Kosher salt and freshly ground
    black pepper

4 tablespoons flour
1 large yellow onion, chopped
4 garlic cloves, chopped
1 cup dry white wine, such as
    Riesling
2¼ cups low-sodium chicken
    broth

½ cup plus 2 tablespoons
    chopped fresh tarragon
    leaves
½ cup Dijon mustard
2 tablespoons unsalted butter

In a Dutch oven or large saucepan, heat the oil over high heat. Season the chicken with 2 teaspoons salt and 1 teaspoon pepper and dust with 2 tablespoons of the flour. Cook the chicken, turning occasionally, until browned on all sides, about 5 minutes. Remove the chicken and set aside on a large plate.

Heat the same pan used for the chicken over medium-high heat. Add the onion and season with 1 teaspoon salt and ½ teaspoon pepper. Cook, stirring frequently, for 4 minutes, until softened. Add the garlic and cook for 30 seconds, until aromatic. Increase the heat to high. Add the wine and scrape up the browned bits that cling to the bottom of the pan with a wooden spoon. Return the chicken pieces to the pan. Add 2 cups of the chicken broth and ½ cup of the tarragon. Bring the mixture to a boil. Reduce the heat, cover the pan, and simmer for 30 minutes, until the chicken is cooked through. Remove the chicken pieces to a platter and tent with foil to keep warm.

In a small bowl, whisk together the remaining ¼ cup chicken broth and the remaining 2 tablespoons flour until smooth. Whisk the flour mixture into the simmering cooking juices. Whisk in the mustard. Bring the mixture to a boil and cook for 5 minutes. Remove from the heat and stir in the butter until smooth. Season to taste with salt and pepper. Serve the sauce over the chicken and garnish with the remaining tarragon.

chicken meunière with tomato and parsley sauce

This chicken dish is a twist on the classic French dish, sole meunière. Thin chicken cutlets get dredged in seasoned flour and then sautéed until golden. The pan juices make an easy flavorful sauce with the addition of tomatoes, olives, capers, lemon zest, and fresh parsley.

serves 4

¼ cup vegetable oil
2 tablespoons unsalted butter, at room temperature
1 cup flour
Kosher salt and freshly ground black pepper
4 (4-ounce) chicken cutlets, pounded ¼ inch thick

2 tablespoons olive oil
4 plum tomatoes, seeded and diced
¼ cup kalamata olives, quartered
2 tablespoons capers, rinsed and drained

⅓ cup dry white wine, such as Pinot Grigio
Grated zest of ½ large lemon
¼ cup chopped fresh flat-leaf parsley leaves

In a large nonstick skillet, heat the vegetable oil and butter over medium-high heat. In a medium bowl, mix the flour, ½ teaspoon salt, and ¼ teaspoon pepper. Season the chicken on both sides with salt and pepper, then dredge in the seasoned flour mixture. Shake off any excess flour. Cook the chicken cutlets for 3 to 5 minutes on each side, until golden and cooked through. Transfer to a platter and keep warm.

Heat the same pan used to cook the chicken over medium-high heat. Add the olive oil, tomatoes, olives, capers, wine, and lemon zest. Scrape up the browned bits that cling to the bottom of the pan with a wooden spoon. Cook for 4 minutes, until the tomatoes start to soften. Stir in the parsley and season to taste with salt and pepper.

Pour the sauce over the chicken and serve.

crispy chicken with rosemary-lemon salt

Chicken tenders are almost universally loved, and I'm certain that this version will continue the affair. I give the frying oil a nice essence of rosemary by dropping in a sprig to release its oils. Then I use the crispy rosemary to make a savory rosemary-lemon salt to season the chicken, which I coat with cornmeal instead of the usual bread crumbs. Store the extra rosemary-lemon salt in an airtight container and use it to add a burst of flavor to meat, fish, and vegetables.

serves 4

Vegetable oil, for frying
1 (6-inch) sprig fresh rosemary
¼ cup plus ¾ teaspoon kosher
    salt
Grated zest of 1 large lemon

1 pound chicken tenders, cut
    into 2-inch pieces
2 garlic cloves, minced
1½ tablespoons chopped fresh
    rosemary leaves

¼ teaspoon freshly ground
    black pepper
½ cup fine cornmeal or instant
    polenta
2 cups marinara sauce, warmed

Heat ¼ inch of oil in a large, high-sided skillet over medium-high heat (the oil is hot enough when a pinch of cornmeal sizzles when added to the pan). Add the rosemary sprig and fry for 30 seconds, until crisp. Using tongs, remove the rosemary sprig and drain on paper towels. Remove the leaves and finely chop to yield 1 tablespoon. Combine with ¼ cup of the salt and half the lemon zest in a small bowl and mix with a fork. Keep the pan over medium-high heat.

In a medium bowl, mix the chicken, garlic, chopped fresh rosemary, remaining lemon zest, remaining ¾ teaspoon salt, and the pepper. Add the cornmeal and toss until the chicken is coated.

Add half of the chicken to the same skillet used to cook the rosemary and fry for 2 to 3 minutes on each side, until golden and crispy and cooked through. Drain on paper towels. Repeat with the remaining chicken, adding more oil to the pan as needed.

Sprinkle the chicken with the rosemary-lemon salt and serve with the warm marinara sauce alongside.

turkey and pancetta pot pies

I created this dish as a Thanksgiving alternative to a roasted turkey when Todd, Jade, and I decided to spend a quiet holiday at home one year with a smaller, simpler meal. If you're more of a traditionalist and can't do without the big bird, then consider this recipe an option for what to do with the leftover turkey (or rotisserie chicken), vegetables, and herbs. Either way, the store-bought pie crust eliminates the mess and stress of making a homemade dough.

serves 6

2 tablespoons olive oil
4 ounces finely diced pancetta (about 1 cup)
1 tablespoon unsalted butter, at room temperature
1 large or 2 small shallots, chopped
2 medium carrots, peeled and diced into ½-inch pieces

1 tablespoon chopped fresh thyme leaves
½ teaspoon kosher salt
½ teaspoon freshly ground black pepper
¼ cup flour
2½ cups low-sodium chicken broth
¼ cup heavy cream

3 cups (about 14 ounces) ½-inch cubed roasted turkey breast meat
1 cup frozen peas, thawed
½ cup frozen corn, thawed
1 (9-inch diameter) unroll-and-bake pie crust
1 egg, beaten

Place an oven rack in the center of the oven. Preheat the oven to 400°F.

In a large saucepan, heat the oil over medium-high heat. Add the pancetta and cook, stirring occasionally, until browned and crispy, about 8 minutes. Transfer the pancetta to a paper towel–lined plate and discard any fat left in the pan. Add the butter, shallots, carrots, and thyme to the pan. Season with the salt and pepper. Cook for 6 to 8 minutes, until the carrots are tender.

Stir in the flour and cook for 1 minute. Increase the heat to high. Add the chicken broth and scrape up the browned bits that cling to the bottom of the pan with a wooden spoon. Cook until the mixture thickens, about 3 minutes. Add the cooked pancetta, the heavy cream, turkey, peas, and corn and season with salt and pepper. Simmer for 3 minutes, until heated through.

Using a ladle, fill 6 (10-ounce) ramekins, each 2½ inches tall and 3½ inches in diameter, with the filling mixture.

Using a 3-inch-round cookie cutter or glass, cut the crust into 6 circles and place one on each ramekin on top of the filling. Using a pastry brush, brush the crusts with the beaten egg.

Bake for 20 to 25 minutes, until the crusts are golden and the filling is bubbling (if the crusts become too dark, cover the pies loosely with aluminum foil). Cool for 5 minutes before serving.

salmon cakes with lemon-caper yogurt sauce

For all the salmon lovers, like me, this one's for you. The salmon cakes can be prepared in an easy three-step process and served at room temperature. I use crushed saltine crackers instead of bread crumbs in the filling and to coat the salmon cakes because they keep their crunch and actually become crunchier as they cook.

serves 4 to 6

salmon cakes

1 (14.75-ounce) can boneless, skinless pink salmon, drained
1 large egg, beaten
1/3 cup chopped fresh chives
26 saltine crackers, crushed (1 1/3 cups)
1/2 cup frozen corn, thawed
1/4 cup mayonnaise, plus more as needed
2 tablespoons Dijon mustard
1 tablespoon capers, rinsed and drained
1 tablespoon grated lemon zest
1 tablespoon fresh lemon juice
3 tablespoons vegetable oil
3 tablespoons unsalted butter, at room temperature

sauce

1/2 cup full-fat plain Greek yogurt
1 1/2 tablespoons capers, rinsed, drained, and chopped
1 tablespoon grated lemon zest
1 tablespoon fresh lemon juice
1/2 teaspoon kosher salt
1/4 teaspoon freshly ground black pepper

for the salmon cakes: Using a fork, flake the salmon into 1/2-inch pieces into a medium bowl. Add the egg, chives, 1/2 cup of the crushed crackers, the corn, mayonnaise, mustard, capers, lemon zest, and lemon juice. Mix gently until just combined. Form into 10 patties, each about 3/4 inch thick (if the mixture is too dry to form into patties, add extra mayonnaise, 1 tablespoon at a time). Carefully coat the patties in the remaining crushed crackers and refrigerate for 20 minutes.

In a large nonstick skillet, heat the oil and butter together over medium heat. Add the salmon patties and cook for 7 to 8 minutes on each side, until golden and crispy. Drain the patties on paper towels.

for the sauce: In a small bowl, mix the yogurt, capers, lemon zest, lemon juice, salt, and pepper.

Arrange the salmon cakes on a platter and serve the sauce alongside.

balsamic-glazed salmon

Buttery salmon needs an accompaniment with a little acidity to cut though the fish's richness. While the salmon roasts in the oven in this recipe, a sweet and savory balsamic glaze simmers on the stovetop. Serve this with Snap Pea and Edamame Sauté (page 209) or over white or brown rice, or even Israeli couscous.

serves 4

¾ cup balsamic vinegar
2 tablespoons maple syrup
1 tablespoon Dijon mustard
1 garlic clove, minced

Vegetable oil cooking spray
4 (6-ounce) center-cut salmon
    fillets, skinned
2 tablespoons olive oil

1 teaspoon kosher salt
½ teaspoon freshly ground
    black pepper

Place an oven rack in the center of the oven. Preheat the oven to 400°F.

In a small saucepan, bring the vinegar, maple syrup, mustard, and garlic to a boil over medium heat. Reduce the heat and simmer until thick, about 12 minutes. Set aside to cool for 5 minutes.

Spray a small baking sheet with vegetable oil. Arrange the salmon fillets in a single layer on the prepared baking sheet. Drizzle both sides of the salmon with olive oil and season with salt and pepper. Roast for 8 to 10 minutes, until the flesh flakes easily when prodded with a fork.

Transfer the salmon to plates and drizzle with the glaze.

broiled tilapia with mustard-chive sauce

When I'm in the mood for a light and healthy dinner, I gravitate to fish and vegetables. I love this broiled tilapia, which cooks quickly. The mustard in the sauce gives the fish a good zing, and served over Carrot and Yam Puree (page 193), this makes a meal that doesn't feel at all like you've compromised.

serves 4

Vegetable oil cooking spray
4 (5- to 6-ounce) tilapia fillets
Olive oil, for drizzling
Kosher salt and freshly ground
    black pepper

¼ cup plain full-fat Greek
    yogurt
2 teaspoons agave nectar or
    honey
1 teaspoon Dijon mustard

¼ cup lemon juice (from 1 large
    lemon)
2 tablespoons chopped fresh
    chives

Preheat a broiler. Spray a small baking sheet or glass baking dish with vegetable oil spray.

Drizzle the tilapia fillets on both sides with olive oil and season with 1 teaspoon salt and ½ teaspoon pepper. Arrange the fillets in a single layer on the prepared baking sheet and broil for 6 to 8 minutes, until cooked through and the flesh flakes easily when prodded with a fork. Set aside to cool slightly.

In a small bowl, mix the yogurt, agave nectar, and mustard until smooth. Whisk in the lemon juice and chives. Season with ½ teaspoon salt and ¼ teaspoon pepper.

Transfer the tilapia to a serving platter and drizzle with the sauce.

grilled fish kebobs with parsley and garlic butter

I use three types of fish for these kebobs, not only for color but also for variations in flavor and texture. For the accompanying flavored butter, I keep it simple; because the fish is pretty mild-tasting, I use only garlic and parsley, which will enhance the flavor of the fish, not overwhelm it. Stir a spoonful of the parsley and garlic butter into some white or brown rice to serve alongside the kebobs.

serves 4 to 6

kebobs

1 (10-ounce) center-cut salmon steak, skinned, cut into ½-inch cubes (about 20 pieces)
1 (10-ounce) center-cut halibut steak, skinned, cut into ½-inch cubes (about 20 pieces)
1 (10-ounce) tuna steak, skinned, cut into ½-inch cubes (about 20 pieces)

½ cup extra-virgin olive oil
Grated zest and juice of 1 large lemon
3 garlic cloves, minced
1 cup chopped fresh flat-leaf parsley leaves
3 tablespoons fresh thyme leaves, coarsely chopped
Kosher salt and freshly ground black pepper

butter

8 tablespoons (1 stick) unsalted butter, at room temperature
2 garlic cloves, minced
2 tablespoons chopped fresh flat-leaf parsley leaves
¾ teaspoon kosher salt
¼ teaspoon freshly ground black pepper

for the kebobs: Put the salmon, halibut, and tuna in a large resealable plastic bag. In a medium bowl, whisk together the olive oil, lemon zest, lemon juice, garlic, parsley, thyme, 1 teaspoon salt, and ½ teaspoon pepper. Pour the mixture over the fish and seal the bag. Refrigerate for 30 minutes.

Thread each of 10 skewers (see Cook's Note) with 2 pieces of salmon, 2 pieces of halibut, and 2 pieces of tuna, alternating the fish on the skewers.

for the butter: In a small bowl, mix the butter, garlic, parsley, salt, and pepper.

Heat a grill pan over medium-high heat or preheat a gas or charcoal grill. Season the kebobs with salt and pepper and grill for 3 to 4 minutes on each side, until opaque.

Arrange the skewers on a platter and serve topped with the butter.

cook's note

I find long metal skewers easiest to use. If you're using wooden skewers, make sure to soak them in water for 30 minutes before using to prevent them from burning on the grill.

change
of pace

change of pace

Sweet and Spicy Greek Meatballs

Vegetables in Red Curry

Chicken Adobo

Thai Turkey Lettuce Cups

Asian Chicken Salad

Asian Quinoa with Salmon

Quinoa with Peas, Potatoes, and Olives

Black Forbidden Rice with Shrimp, Peaches, and Snap Peas

Chicken with Peruvian Chile Sauce

Tofu with Miso Vinaigrette, Mushrooms, and Edamame

Spicy Mint Beef

Citrus Rice Salad with Tofu

Tilapia Fish Tacos with Arugula

sweet and spicy greek meatballs

This is my spin on a Greek meatball, flavored with garlic, mint, oregano, and cinnamon. I also add cumin for warmth and cayenne for heat, and use couscous instead of bread crumbs. Form these gently to keep the meatballs light and moist. Make some extra couscous to serve alongside.

serves 4 to 6

1 pound ground lamb or 80% lean ground beef
1 cup cooked and cooled couscous (see Cook's Note)
3 scallions, white and pale green parts, chopped
2 garlic cloves, chopped
1 large egg, at room temperature, beaten

¼ cup chopped fresh flat-leaf parsley leaves, plus more for serving
5 tablespoons olive oil
3 tablespoons dried mint
1½ tablespoons dried oregano
1½ teaspoons ground cumin

2 tablespoons ground cinnamon
2 teaspoons kosher salt
½ teaspoon freshly ground black pepper
½ teaspoon cayenne pepper
2 cups marinara sauce
2 cinnamon sticks

In a large bowl, mix the lamb, couscous, scallions, garlic, egg, parsley, 2 tablespoons of the olive oil, the mint, oregano, cumin, 1 tablespoon of the ground cinnamon, the salt, black pepper, and cayenne. Form into 14 to 16 meatballs 2 inches in diameter.

Heat the remaining 3 tablespoons olive oil in a large nonstick skillet over medium-high heat. Add the meatballs and cook until they are browned on all sides, about 6 minutes. Add the marinara sauce, remaining 1 tablespoon ground cinnamon, and the cinnamon sticks to the pan. Bring the sauce to a boil and then reduce the heat so that it simmers. Cook, turning occasionally, until the meatballs are cooked through, 10 to 12 minutes. Discard the cinnamon sticks.

Transfer the meatballs and sauce to a serving bowl. Garnish with chopped parsley and serve.

cook's note

To make 1 cup cooked couscous, bring ½ cup water or stock to a boil. Add ⅓ cup uncooked couscous and cover the pan. Remove the pan from the heat and allow the mixture to sit for 5 minutes, until all the liquid has been absorbed. Fluff with a fork and allow to cool.

vegetables in red curry

It's kind of fun to mix things up on a weeknight with a little spice. Creamy coconut milk gets a kick from spicy chile and Thai basil. Loaded with veggies and served over brown rice, this is my kind of Thai dish.

serves 4 to 6

2 (13.5-ounce) cans coconut milk

¼ cup (2 ounces) red curry paste (see Cook's Note), such as Mae Ploy

1 small (8 ounces) russet potato, peeled and cut into ¼-inch pieces

2 carrots, peeled and sliced ¼ inch thick

1 small onion, chopped

½ red bell pepper, cored, seeded, and chopped

1 (15-ounce) can baby corn, rinsed and drained

1 Thai or serrano chile, stemmed and thinly sliced

5 sprigs basil, preferably Thai, with stems

3 kaffir lime leaves or grated zest of 1 lime

1 tablespoon Thai fish sauce

4 ounces sugar snap peas, trimmed and halved

¼ cup chopped fresh basil leaves, preferably Thai

In a large saucepan, bring the coconut milk and curry paste to a boil over medium-high heat, stirring constantly until smooth, about 1 minute. Add the potato, carrots, onion, bell pepper, corn, chile, basil sprigs, lime leaves, and fish sauce. Bring the mixture to a simmer. Lower the heat, cover the pan, and simmer for 30 minutes.

Remove the lid and continue to simmer until the curry is thick and the vegetables are tender, about 3 minutes. Add the snap peas and simmer for 2 minutes.

Remove the lime leaves and the basil sprigs. Garnish with the chopped basil before serving.

cook's note

If you prefer a milder heat, replace the red curry paste with an equal amount of yellow curry paste.

chicken adobo

The word *adobo* is a Spanish term for "marinade," and tart adobo sauces are common in South American dishes. In this Filipino-inspired dish, I use aromatic bay leaves, white wine vinegar, soy sauce, and garlic to stand up to flavorful chicken drumsticks. Serve alongside some herbed white rice.

serves 4 to 6

¼ cup vegetable oil
12 chicken drumsticks
Kosher salt and freshly ground
    black pepper
2 cups low-sodium chicken
    broth
1 cup white wine vinegar

1 cup low-sodium soy sauce
½ cup light brown sugar
4 garlic cloves, chopped
¾ teaspoon crushed red
    pepper flakes
2 dried bay leaves
3 tablespoons arrowroot

2 tablespoons fresh lime juice
    (from 2 large limes)
2 tablespoons chopped fresh
    flat-leaf parsley or cilantro
    leaves
Lime wedges

In a 12-inch nonstick, high-sided skillet, heat the oil over medium-high heat. Season the chicken with salt and pepper. Add the chicken to the pan and brown on all sides, about 5 minutes.

In a medium bowl, combine the chicken broth, vinegar, soy sauce, sugar, garlic, red pepper flakes, and bay leaves. Whisk until the sugar has dissolved.

Pour the liquid into the skillet with the chicken and bring to a boil, scraping up with a wooden spoon the browned bits that stick to the bottom of the pan. Reduce the heat and simmer, turning the chicken occasionally, for 35 minutes, until cooked through.

Remove the chicken from the cooking liquid and arrange on a serving platter. Discard the bay leaves. Whisk the arrowroot and lime juice into the cooking liquid and bring to a boil. Cook until the mixture thickens, about 5 minutes. Season to taste with salt and pepper.

Pour the sauce over the chicken or serve alongside as a dipping sauce. Sprinkle the chicken with chopped parsley and garnish with lime wedges.

thai turkey lettuce cups

Todd loves Thai food, and to indulge him on occasion, I've learned to cook a few dishes that taste very similar to the real deal yet come together quickly. These lettuce cups are filled with ground turkey, but you can use ground chicken, beef, or pork. The mint and lemongrass give it freshness, as does the tangy dressing. These are great with sticky rice.

serves 4

⅓ cup fresh lime juice (from about 5 limes)
3 tablespoons fresh lemon juice (from 1 large lemon)
2 tablespoons Thai fish sauce
2 tablespoons honey
3 tablespoons canola oil
½ red onion, diced

3 small shallots, thinly sliced
1 (4-inch) piece of lemongrass, minced (about ¼ cup)
1 Thai or serrano chile, stemmed and thinly sliced
1½ pounds ground turkey, preferably dark meat

Kosher salt and freshly ground black pepper
½ cup chopped fresh mint leaves
1 head butter lettuce, leaves separated

In a small bowl, whisk together the lime juice, lemon juice, fish sauce, and honey.

In a large skillet, heat the oil over medium heat. Add the onion, shallots, lemongrass, and chile. Cook until the vegetables begin to soften, about 5 minutes. Add the turkey and season with salt. Cook, stirring frequently, until the meat and vegetables are cooked through, about 5 minutes.

Add the dressing to the pan and cook for 2 minutes. Remove from the heat and stir in the mint. Season to taste with salt and pepper.

Spoon the turkey mixture onto the lettuce leaves and serve.

asian chicken salad

This is my take on a Chinese chicken salad, something I could eat every day. I love the crunch and the balance of sweet, salty, and tart.

serves 4 to 6

1 large carrot, peeled
3 cups shredded napa cabbage (from 1 small head)
3 cups shredded romaine lettuce (from 1 small head)
1 small red bell pepper, cored, seeded, and thinly sliced
2 tablespoons fresh basil leaves, preferably Thai, or fresh mint leaves, chopped

2 cups thinly sliced store-bought rotisserie chicken (about 2 small chicken breasts)
½ cup slivered almonds, toasted (see Cook's Note)
1 tablespoon toasted white or black sesame seeds
¼ cup peanut or vegetable oil

2 tablespoons low-sodium soy sauce
2 tablespoons rice vinegar
½ teaspoon sugar
Kosher salt and freshly ground black pepper, optional
½ cup chow mein noodles

Using a vegetable peeler, shave the carrot into a large salad bowl. Add the cabbage, lettuce, bell pepper, basil, chicken, almonds, and sesame seeds.

In a small bowl, whisk together the oil, soy sauce, vinegar, and sugar until smooth. Season to taste with salt and pepper, if desired.

Pour the dressing over the salad and toss well. Garnish with the chow mein noodles and serve.

cook's note

To toast the slivered almonds, arrange them in a single layer on a baking sheet. Bake in a preheated 350°F oven for 8 to 10 minutes, until lightly golden. Cool completely before using.

asian quinoa with salmon

I love how quinoa pops when you bite into it—it's good for you and tastes great, too! I up the natural nutrition by adding simple ingredients, like a combination of fresh herbs and flaked salmon, making this an easy and healthy meal.

serves 4

3 cups low-sodium chicken
  broth
1½ cups quinoa
2 teaspoons Chinese 5-spice
  powder
¼ cup seasoned rice wine
  vinegar

2 tablespoons grapeseed oil
2 tablespoons sesame oil
1 tablespoon low-sodium soy
  sauce
Kosher salt and freshly ground
  black pepper

1 (14.75-ounce) can boneless,
  skinless pink salmon, drained
¼ cup chopped fresh cilantro
  leaves

In a medium saucepan, bring the chicken broth, quinoa, and 5-spice powder to a boil over medium-high heat. Reduce the heat, cover the pan, and simmer until all the liquid is absorbed, 12 to 15 minutes. Set aside to cool for 10 minutes.

In a small bowl, whisk together the vinegar, grapeseed oil, sesame oil, soy sauce, and ½ teaspoon salt until smooth.

Put the quinoa, salmon, and cilantro in a serving bowl. Pour the dressing on top and toss until all the ingredients are coated. Season to taste with salt and pepper, and serve.

quinoa with peas, potatoes, and olives

Quinoa is my new favorite—it's a great high-protein substitute for rice. I saw every color, shape, size, taste, and texture of potatoes in Peru and especially love the purple ones. The herby oregano dressing for this hearty salad marries the flavors to create a wonderful dish.

serves 6 to 8

12 ounces purple Peruvian potatoes, cut into ½-inch pieces
4 cups low-sodium chicken broth
2 cups quinoa
3 garlic cloves, peeled and smashed

2 cups (8 ounces) frozen peas, thawed
½ cup pitted medium black olives
⅓ cup chopped fresh oregano leaves
¼ cup extra-virgin olive oil

¼ cup agave nectar
3 tablespoons fresh lime juice (from 2 to 3 large limes)
1 teaspoon kosher salt
¼ teaspoon freshly ground black pepper

Put the potatoes in a medium saucepan with enough salted cold water to cover by 2 inches. Bring to a boil over medium-high heat. Cook until tender, 12 to 15 minutes. Drain in a colander and set aside to cool.

Meanwhile, in a large saucepan or Dutch oven, bring the chicken broth, quinoa, and garlic to a boil over medium-high heat. Reduce the heat, cover the pot, and simmer until the liquid has been absorbed and the quinoa is tender, 12 to 15 minutes.

Remove from the heat and let rest for 5 minutes. Remove the garlic and discard. Using a fork, fluff the quinoa and transfer to a large serving bowl. Add the peas and the cooked potatoes.

In a food processor, combine the olives, oregano, oil, agave nectar, lime juice, salt, and pepper. Process until chunky.

Pour the dressing over the quinoa and toss well to coat.

black forbidden rice with shrimp, peaches, and snap peas

Black "forbidden rice" takes its name from ancient times, when reportedly only China's emperor was allowed to eat it—no one else. This beautiful rice actually has more of a purple color once it's cooked. I serve it with pan-fried shrimp, sautéed snap peas, and peaches, as well as a tangy dressing. It's sweet, savory, and colorful. If you have trouble finding black rice, go ahead and substitute brown, basmati, or jasmine rice.

serves 4 to 6

2 cups black forbidden rice
1 (1½-inch) piece fresh ginger, peeled and finely chopped
Kosher salt and freshly ground black pepper
¼ cup plus 3 tablespoons grapeseed oil

1½ pounds peeled and deveined large shrimp
2½ cups (8 ounces) sugar snap peas, trimmed and cut into 1-inch pieces
3 peaches, stones removed, cut into ¼-inch-thick slices (see Cook's Note)

¼ cup seasoned rice vinegar
3 tablespoons honey
1 tablespoon soy sauce

In a medium saucepan, bring 3½ cups water, the rice, ginger, and 2 teaspoons salt to a boil over medium heat. Reduce the heat, cover the pan, and simmer until the rice is tender, about 30 minutes. Remove from the heat and set aside for 5 minutes. Fluff with a fork and transfer to a large serving bowl.

Meanwhile, in a large nonstick skillet, heat 2 tablespoons of the grapeseed oil over medium-high heat. Add the shrimp and season with salt and pepper. Cook, stirring frequently, until the shrimp are cooked through and opaque, 4 to 5 minutes. Remove the shrimp and set aside to cool. Using paper towels, wipe the pan dry.

In the same pan, heat 1 tablespoon of the oil over medium-high heat. Add the snap peas and cook, stirring frequently, until slightly soft, about 2 minutes. Add the peach slices and cook for 2 minutes. Transfer the peas and peaches to the serving bowl.

In a medium bowl, whisk together the vinegar, the remaining ¼ cup oil, honey, and soy sauce until smooth. Pour the dressing over the rice mixture. Add the shrimp and toss well. Serve warm or at room temperature.

cook's note

Slightly underripe peaches will hold up better to the heat while cooking. If your peaches are fully ripe, sauté for just a minute to a minute and a half.

chicken with peruvian chile sauce

I went on a trip to Peru with Oxfam America, a charity I love to support. My experience not only gave me a great opportunity to learn about the food and farmers there but it also inspired me to try to re-create some of the amazing dishes I ate. This Peruvian chile sauce is authentic in its use of slightly spicy yellow peppers, which are a beautiful color. I add a little Parmesan cheese for thickness and a nice salty bite.

serves 4 to 6

Vegetable oil cooking spray
1 (4- to 5-pound) chicken, cut into 8 pieces
4 tablespoons vegetable oil
Kosher salt and freshly ground black pepper
1 slice whole wheat sandwich bread, crust removed, torn into ½-inch pieces

¾ cup half-and-half
1 large or 2 small shallots, sliced
2 garlic cloves, crushed
1 cup low-sodium chicken broth
2 cups (8 ounces) crumbled queso fresco or mild feta cheese
½ cup grated Parmesan cheese

½ cup plus ⅓ cup chopped walnuts, toasted (see Cook's Note)
1 tablespoon aji amarillo paste (see Cook's Note, page 156)
½ teaspoon turmeric
½ tablespoon chopped fresh cilantro or flat-leaf parsley leaves

Place an oven rack in the center of the oven. Preheat the oven to 400°F.

Spray a heavy baking sheet with vegetable oil. Rub the chicken on all sides with 2 tablespoons of the oil and season with salt and pepper. Arrange the chicken pieces in a single layer on the prepared baking sheet. Bake for 35 to 45 minutes, until a meat thermometer inserted into the thickest part of each piece of chicken registers 160°F. Let the chicken rest for 15 minutes.

Meanwhile, put the bread and half-and-half in the bowl of a food processor. Allow the bread to soak up the liquid, about 10 minutes.

In a 10-inch nonstick skillet, heat the remaining 2 tablespoons oil over medium-high heat. Add the shallot and cook, stirring occasionally, until soft, 3 to 4 minutes. Add the garlic and cook for 30 seconds, until aromatic. Cool slightly and add to the food processor with the soaked bread. Add the broth, cheese, ½ cup walnuts, aji amarillo paste, and turmeric. Blend until smooth.

cook's note

To toast the walnuts, arrange in a single layer on a baking sheet. Bake in a preheated 350°F oven for 6 to 8 minutes, until lightly toasted. Cool completely before using.

recipe continues

Pour the sauce back into the skillet and bring to a simmer over medium heat. Simmer for 5 minutes, until slightly thickened. Season to taste with salt.

Spoon the sauce onto a platter and arrange the chicken on top. Sprinkle with the remaining ⅓ cup walnuts and the cilantro and serve.

cook's note

Aji amarillo paste, a creamy puree of the bright yellow-orange spicy pepper, can be found online, in Latin markets, or in the Latin section of grocery stores. If you can't find it, core and seed an orange bell pepper. Cut it into 2-inch pieces and puree in a blender or food processor with ½ habanero pepper (with seeds) and ½ teaspoon kosher salt. Drain in a sieve, and using the back of a rubber spatula, gently push on the puree to release any liquid. Use 2 tablespoons of the puree in place of the aji amarillo paste.

tofu with miso vinaigrette, mushrooms, and edamame

I love a succulent piece of buttery cod broiled with a miso sauce—it's a perfect harmony of sweet, tangy, and salty. Instead of offering another fish recipe, though, I developed this one for the tofu lovers and vegetarians (and maybe even the meat eaters!). It's a colorful Japanese-inspired dish that will transport your weeknight dinner to a whole new level of flavor. Serve over steamed rice.

serves 4

vinaigrette

½ cup white miso paste (see Cook's Note)
⅓ cup toasted sesame oil
⅓ cup seasoned rice vinegar
¼ cup honey
¼ cup soy sauce
1 (2-inch) piece fresh ginger, peeled and chopped
2 garlic cloves, smashed

tofu

2 (12-ounce) containers of extra-firm tofu, drained and patted dry
4 tablespoons toasted sesame oil
5 cups (10 ounces) thinly sliced stemmed shiitake mushrooms

1 cup (about 8 ounces) shelled edamame beans
2 scallions, white and pale green parts, thinly sliced
1 tablespoon black or toasted sesame seeds

for the vinaigrette: In a blender, combine the miso paste, sesame oil, vinegar, honey, soy sauce, ginger, and garlic. Blend until smooth.

for the tofu: Cut the tofu in half crosswise. Cut each half horizontally, through the side, to make 8 rectangles of tofu, each 3½ x 2¼ inches and ½ inch thick. Brush the tofu with 3 tablespoons of the vinaigrette. Let marinate for 15 minutes.

In a large nonstick skillet, heat 2 tablespoons of the oil over medium-high heat. Add the tofu and cook for 4 to 5 minutes on each side, until golden. Remove the tofu, placing 2 slices on each of four serving plates.

In the same pan, heat the remaining 2 tablespoons oil over high heat. Add the mushrooms and 2 tablespoons of the vinaigrette. Cook, stirring frequently, until tender, about 5 minutes. Add the edamame beans and cook until warmed through, about 1 minute.

Spoon the mushroom mixture over the tofu and drizzle with the vinaigrette. Garnish with the chopped scallions and sesame seeds.

cook's note

Miso paste can be found in many well-stocked supermarkets these days. If you can't find it, substitute creamy peanut butter and reduce the amount of soy sauce to 3 tablespoons.

spicy mint beef

Thai food in Los Angeles is quite popular, and there's even an area called Thai Town with lots of authentic restaurants and shops. This dish is fast and simple to prepare and bursting with flavor. Serve it over steamed rice to soak up all of the delicious sauce.

serves 4

3 tablespoons vegetable or canola oil
4 garlic cloves, minced
3 Thai or serrano chiles, cored and thinly sliced
3 small shallots, thinly sliced
1 red bell pepper, cored, seeded, and thinly sliced

¼ cup Thai fish sauce
2 tablespoons sweet soy sauce (see Cook's Note)
2 tablespoons black soy sauce (see Cook's Note)
1 tablespoon chili paste in oil, or Sriracha sauce

1 (1-pound) sirloin steak, very thinly sliced
1½ cups chopped fresh basil leaves, preferably Thai
1 cup fresh mint leaves

In a large skillet, heat the vegetable oil over medium-high heat. Add the garlic and chiles and cook until aromatic, about 30 seconds. Add the shallots and bell pepper and cook for 1 minute. Add the fish sauce, sweet soy sauce, black soy sauce, and chili paste. Bring the mixture to a low simmer and cook, stirring frequently, until the vegetables are tender, about 2 minutes.

Add the steak and cook, stirring frequently, for about 5 minutes for medium. Remove the skillet from the heat and stir in the basil and mint until wilted.

cook's note

In place of the sweet and black soy sauces, if you do not have them, use ¼ cup regular soy sauce mixed with ¼ cup honey or sugar.

citrus rice salad with tofu

I love rice. I love citrus. And I love salads. This recipe combines all three into one perfect dish, with Asian-Indian flair. The almonds, orange and lemon, scallions, and soy sauce bring to mind ingredients you'd find in a Chinese dish, while the basmati rice and cumin are characteristically Indian. If you have leftover cooked rice, use it here; you'll need 4 cups.

serves 4 to 6

rice salad

4 cups low-sodium chicken broth

2 tablespoons extra-virgin olive oil

½ teaspoon kosher salt

2 cups brown basmati rice, rinsed

1 cup thinly sliced scallions, white and pale green parts

¾ cup chopped fresh flat-leaf parsley

Grated zest and juice of 1 medium orange, plus more juice if needed

Grated zest and juice of 1 large lemon, plus more juice if needed

½ cup sliced almonds, toasted (see Cook's Note)

tofu

1 cup extra-virgin olive oil

½ cup fresh orange juice

⅓ cup fresh lemon juice (about 2 large lemons)

¼ cup soy sauce

2 tablespoons honey

1 tablespoon ground cumin

Kosher salt and freshly ground black pepper

1 (12-ounce) container extra-firm tofu, drained and patted dry

for the rice salad: In a medium saucepan, bring the chicken broth, the oil, and the salt to a boil over medium-high heat. Stir in the rice, cover the saucepan, and lower the heat. Simmer until all the liquid has been absorbed and the rice is tender, about 40 minutes. Remove the pan from the heat and let rest, covered, for 5 minutes. Using a fork, fluff the rice and then transfer to a large serving bowl. Add the scallions, parsley, orange zest, half of the lemon zest, and half of the almonds. Toss well.

for the tofu: In a blender, combine the olive oil, orange juice, lemon juice, soy sauce, honey, cumin, 1½ teaspoons salt, and 1 teaspoon pepper. Blend until smooth. Pour half of the vinaigrette into a resealable plastic bag; reserve the remaining vinaigrette. Add the tofu and marinate for 10 minutes.

Drain off the marinade into a large nonstick skillet over medium-high heat. Bring to a boil and then add the tofu. Cook, stirring gently, until the tofu is warmed through, about 5 minutes.

Pour the reserved vinaigrette and cooked tofu over the rice and toss gently until coated. Season to taste with salt and pepper. Garnish the dish with the remaining lemon zest and almonds.

cook's note

To toast the almonds, arrange in a single layer on a baking sheet. Bake in a preheated 350°F oven for 5 to 7 minutes, until lightly toasted. Cool completely before using.

tilapia fish tacos with arugula

With a melting pot of influences, these fish tacos use store-bought corn tortillas to hold a wonderful mix of tilapia—a freshwater white fish—sweet ripe mango, creamy avocado, and peppery arugula. A lightly spicy wasabi cream is the finishing touch that makes each bite sing.

serves 4

⅓ cup plus 4 tablespoons olive oil

6 tilapia fillets (about 1 pound total), cut into ¾-inch pieces

Kosher salt and freshly ground black pepper

¼ cup fresh lime juice (from about 4 limes)

2 avocados, peeled, seeded, and cut into ½-inch cubes

2 mangoes, peeled, seeded, and cut into ½-inch cubes

6 scallions, white and pale green parts, finely chopped

4 packed cups (4 ounces) baby arugula, coarsely chopped

3 tablespoons chopped fresh cilantro leaves

1 cup crème fraîche or sour cream

2 tablespoons wasabi powder

8 (6-inch) corn tortillas

In a large, nonstick skillet, heat 3 tablespoons of the olive oil over medium-high heat. Drizzle the tilapia fillets with 1 tablespoon of the olive oil and season both sides with 1 tablespoon salt and 1 teaspoon pepper. Arrange half of the fish in a single layer in the pan and cook for 2 to 3 minutes on each side, until the flesh is flaky and cooked through. Repeat with the remaining fish. Set aside to cool slightly.

In a medium bowl, whisk together the remaining ⅓ cup olive oil, the lime juice, and 1 teaspoon salt. Add the avocados, mangoes, scallions, arugula, and cilantro. Toss until all the ingredients are coated.

In a small bowl, mix the crème fraîche, wasabi powder, and ½ teaspoon salt until smooth.

To warm the tortillas, heat them in batches in a dry skillet or place over a flame, turning occasionally, for about 30 seconds on each side until warm.

Divide the mango-avocado salad among the centers of the tortillas. Top with the fish and 1 to 2 teaspoons of the wasabi crème fraîche and serve.

breakfast for dinner

breakfast for dinner

Breakfast Tart with Pancetta
and Green Onions

Almond Pancakes

Peach and Cherry Frittata

Eggs Florentine

Fig and Brie Panini

Crepes with Peanut Butter and Jam

Crispy Breakfast Pita

Savory Polenta with Sausage
and Dried Cranberries

Smoked Salmon Crostata

Baked Potatoes with Sausage
and Arugula

breakfast tart with pancetta and green onions

This is similar to a quiche—rich and cheesy—or even an omelet on toast, but so much better! However you think of it, definitely think of it for dinner.

serves 6 to 8

Butter, for the pan
Flour, for the pan
1 (9-inch) unroll-and-bake
    refrigerated pie crust
1 large egg white, lightly beaten
2 teaspoons vegetable oil

3 ounces pancetta, cut into
    ¼-inch pieces
5 large eggs, at room
    temperature
½ cup (4 ounces) mascarpone
    cheese, at room temperature

2 cups (8 ounces) shredded
    Gruyère cheese
3 scallions, white and pale green
    parts, thinly sliced
½ teaspoon kosher salt
½ teaspoon freshly ground
    black pepper

Place an oven rack in the center of the oven. Preheat the oven to 400°F.

Butter and flour the bottom and sides of a 9-inch tart pan with a removable bottom. Unroll the pie crust and gently press into the bottom and sides of the pan. Trim any excess from the top.

With the tines of a fork, prick the bottom of the pastry. Using a pastry brush, brush the crust with the beaten egg white. Put the pan on a baking sheet and bake for 10 minutes, until the egg white has set. Let cool for 10 minutes.

Meanwhile, in a medium skillet, heat the oil over medium-high heat. Add the pancetta and cook, stirring frequently, for 6 to 8 minutes, until browned and crispy. Drain on a paper towel–lined plate.

In a medium bowl, lightly beat the eggs. Whisk in the mascarpone, Gruyère, scallions, salt, pepper, and the pancetta. Pour into the cooled crust and bake for about 18 minutes, until the mixture has set and the top is golden.

Cool the tart for 10 to 15 minutes and then remove from the pan. Cut the tart into wedges and serve warm or at room temperature.

almond pancakes

Todd and Jade absolutely love pancakes, so it's not uncommon for them to eat pancakes any time of day, dinner included. To make the pancakes a little special, I add mascarpone cheese, almond extract, and almond paste to the pancake batter, giving it a wonderful amaretto-like flavor. Make sure the almond paste is at room temperature so that it will break down when it's added to the food processor—and be sure to leave a few chunks in the final batter because those bites of almond are really delicious.

makes 16 pancakes; serves 6

½ cup (4 ounces) mascarpone
    cheese, at room temperature
1 tablespoon sugar
2 teaspoons pure almond
    extract

1 teaspoon pure vanilla extract
2 cups buttermilk pancake mix,
    such as Krusteaz
4 ounces (½ cup) almond paste,
    cut into ¼-inch pieces

Unsalted butter, for the griddle
Maple syrup
Fresh raspberries

In a food processor, combine the mascarpone cheese, 1½ cups water, the sugar, almond extract, and vanilla. Process until the mixture is smooth. Add the pancake mix and pulse until just combined. Add the almond paste and pulse once to incorporate.

Heat a griddle or a large nonstick skillet over medium-low heat. Grease the griddle or skillet with butter. Working in batches, pour ¼ cup of batter per pancake onto the griddle and cook for about 1½ minutes on each side, until golden.

Arrange the pancakes on plates and serve topped with maple syrup and fresh raspberries.

peach and cherry frittata

I love this sweet and savory frittata, or baked omelet. Because it has fruit in it, it's definitely a little different and special on a weeknight. The flavors of the peaches and cherries are complemented by the woody essence of thyme and tanginess of goat cheese.

serves 6

8 ounces frozen peaches, thawed and drained
8 ounces frozen cherries, thawed and drained
6 large eggs, at room temperature

¼ cup whole milk
⅓ cup sugar
1 tablespoon chopped fresh thyme leaves
½ teaspoon kosher salt

1 tablespoon vegetable or canola oil
⅓ cup (about 2 ounces) crumbled fresh goat cheese
Maple syrup, for serving

Place an oven rack in the center of the oven. Preheat the oven to 350°F.

Put the thawed peaches and cherries on a paper towel–lined plate to remove any excess juices.

In a medium bowl, whisk the eggs, milk, sugar, thyme, and salt until smooth. Stir in the fruit mixture.

Heat the oil in a 10-inch oven-safe nonstick skillet over medium heat. Pour in the egg mixture and, using a wooden spoon, carefully distribute the fruit evenly in the pan. Sprinkle the cheese over the top and cook without stirring for 5 to 6 minutes, or until the edges start to set. Transfer the skillet to the oven and bake until the frittata is slightly puffed and the egg mixture has set, 25 to 30 minutes. Cool for 5 minutes.

Using a silicone or rubber spatula, loosen the edge of the frittata and slide onto a platter. Cut into wedges and serve with maple syrup.

eggs florentine

Traditionally, eggs florentine have some kind of toasted bread, topped with wilted spinach, a poached egg, and cheese sauce. But I add a couple spins on that—crispy prosciutto being one of them and creamed spinach, which is much easier to make than a cheese sauce. You can use whatever bread you like. I prefer English muffins so the creamed spinach can soak into those nooks and crannies.

serves 4

Vegetable oil cooking spray
4 thin slices prosciutto
3 tablespoons olive oil
1 small onion, finely chopped
3 garlic cloves, minced
6 packed cups (6 ounces) baby
  spinach

¼ teaspoon ground nutmeg
½ cup heavy cream
⅔ cup grated pecorino romano
  cheese
Kosher salt and freshly ground
  black pepper

1 tablespoon fresh lemon juice
4 eggs, at room temperature
  (see Cook's Notes)
2 English muffins, halved
  crosswise (see Cook's Notes)

Place an oven rack in the center of the oven. Preheat the oven to 400°F.

Spray a baking sheet with vegetable oil. Arrange the prosciutto in a single layer on the prepared baking sheet. Bake until crispy, 6 to 8 minutes. Cool completely and then crumble into small pieces. Keep the oven on.

In a medium skillet, heat the oil over medium-high heat. Add the onion and cook, stirring frequently, until soft, about 5 minutes. Add the garlic and cook until fragrant, about 30 seconds. Add the spinach and nutmeg and cook for 1 to 2 minutes, until the spinach has wilted. Add the heavy cream and bring the mixture to a simmer. Cook for 5 minutes, stirring occasionally, until the mixture thickens slightly. Remove the pan from the heat and stir in the cheese, 2 teaspoons salt, and ½ teaspoon pepper. Cover to keep warm.

Fill a small saucepan with 3 inches of water. Add 1 tablespoon salt and the lemon juice. Bring the water to a simmer over medium heat. Crack an egg into a small bowl or cup, taking care not to break the yolk. Slowly slide the egg into the water. Using a wooden spoon, carefully stir the water around the egg. Cook for 2 to 2½ minutes, until the white has set and the yolk is still soft. Using a slotted spoon, remove the egg from the water and drain on paper towels. Repeat with the remaining eggs.

cook's notes

The poached eggs can be made ahead of time. Store them in a bowl of water in the refrigerator. Reheat by placing in simmering water for 30 seconds.

The English muffins can be browned, alternatively, in a toaster or toaster oven.

Meanwhile, place the muffins on a baking sheet and bake for 5 to 6 minutes, until lightly browned and crisp.

To serve, place an English muffin half on each of four plates. Spoon one-quarter of the spinach on top. Set a poached egg on top of the spinach and sprinkle with the crumbled prosciutto.

fig and brie panini

Sandwiches can be so dry and boring, which is why I often turn to a really good melting cheese and an equally delicious spread, whether a mayo, mustard, or this delicious fig jam. The compression of the sandwich in the panini press allows all of the ingredients to meld, making each bite an amazing balance of savory, sweet, and gooey. I'd say it's a pretty good meal to end the day.

serves 4

Vegetable oil cooking spray
16 thin slices pancetta
½ cup sugar
12 dried Black Mission figs, halved

3 tablespoons brandy or apple juice
½ cup hazelnuts, toasted (see Cook's Notes)

4 ciabatta rolls, halved lengthwise
6 ounces Brie, rind removed, cut into 4 slices (see Cook's Notes)

Place an oven rack in the center of the oven. Preheat the oven to 400°F.

Spray two baking sheets with vegetable oil. Arrange the pancetta in a single layer on each baking sheet. Bake until golden and crispy, 6 to 8 minutes.

Meanwhile, in a small saucepan, combine ½ cup water, the sugar, figs, and brandy over medium heat. Bring to a boil, reduce the heat, and simmer, stirring occasionally, for 5 minutes or until the sugar has dissolved. Remove the pan from the heat and allow to cool slightly, about 10 minutes.

Pour the fig mixture into a food processor and add the hazelnuts. Blend until smooth and thick.

Preheat a panini press (see Cook's Notes).

Spread the bottom half of each roll with the fig jam. Place 4 slices of cooked pancetta on top and add a slice of cheese. Place the top half of the roll on top of the cheese. Grill until the bread is toasted and the cheese has melted, about 5 minutes. Cool slightly and serve.

cook's notes

To toast the hazelnuts, arrange in a single layer on a baking sheet. Bake in a preheated 350°F oven for 8 to 10 minutes, until lightly toasted. Cool completely before using.

For easier slicing, freeze the cheese for 15 minutes.

If you don't have a panini press or indoor grill, use a grill pan. Preheat it before adding the sandwiches, weighting them down on top with a heavy pan, such as a cast-iron skillet. Be sure to flip the sandwiches halfway through cooking to brown the second side.

crepes with peanut butter and jam

Making crepes can seem like an intimidating task, but this recipe proves just how simple they are. The batter is made in a blender and cooked in a regular nonstick skillet. The beauty of crepes is that you can fill them with virtually anything: cheese, jam, mushrooms, chocolate, and so on. I've gone for a simple yet classic peanut butter and jelly combination that Jade in particular adores. The crepes are lighter and less chewy than bread; rolled into a tube shape, they are very easy for kids to handle.

makes 8 crepes; serves 4

4 large eggs
1 cup whole milk
½ cup all-purpose flour
1 tablespoon sugar
⅛ teaspoon fine sea salt

3 tablespoons unsalted butter, cut into 10 cubes
⅓ cup creamy peanut butter, at room temperature
½ cup strawberry or raspberry jam

½ cup (2 ounces) fresh blueberries
Confectioners' sugar, for dusting

In a blender, combine the eggs, milk, flour, sugar, and salt. Blend until the mixture forms a smooth batter.

Heat a 10-inch nonstick skillet over medium-low heat. Melt 1 cube of butter in the pan. Add ¼ cup of batter and quickly tilt the pan to form an even coating of batter on the bottom of the pan. Cook for 1 minute, until set and slightly browned. Using a heat-resistant spatula, carefully loosen the sides and gently flip the crepe over. Cook for 1 minute. Repeat with the remaining batter and butter, stacking the crepes on top of each other on a plate as they are ready. You should have 8 or 9 crepes total.

Add 1 tablespoon of peanut butter to each crepe, and using the back of a spoon, spread evenly over the crepes leaving a ½-inch border. Spread 2 teaspoons of jam over the peanut butter. Line 5 to 6 blueberries along the center of each crepe. Fold the crepe in half over the blueberries. Fold the two ends inwards and continue to roll into a tube shape. Repeat with the remaining ingredients.

Cut each crepe in half horizontally and arrange on a platter. Dust with confectioners' sugar and serve.

crispy breakfast pita

This is a twist on a *piadina,* an Italian flatbread. For weeknight ease, instead of making a dough, I use store-bought pitas as the base. They get topped with a creamy mascarpone spread, a salty bite of prosciutto, a lightly dressed arugula salad, and a fried egg.

serves 6

6 (6-inch) pita breads
Extra-virgin olive oil
6 large eggs
¾ cup (6 ounces) mascarpone
   cheese

Grated zest of ½ large lemon
Kosher salt and freshly ground
   black pepper
3 tablespoons fresh lemon juice

3 packed cups (3 ounces)
   arugula or baby spinach
8 ounces thinly sliced prosciutto

Heat a grill pan over medium-high heat or preheat a gas or charcoal grill. Brush each side of the pita breads with ½ teaspoon olive oil and grill for 2 to 3 minutes on each side, until crisp. Remove from the grill and cool slightly.

In a large skillet, heat 1 tablespoon olive oil over medium-high heat. Crack the eggs directly into the pan and cook until the egg whites are set, 2 to 3 minutes.

Combine the mascarpone cheese, lemon zest, ½ teaspoon salt, and ½ teaspoon pepper in a small bowl.

In a medium bowl, whisk together 3 tablespoons olive oil, the lemon juice, 1 teaspoon salt, and ½ teaspoon pepper until smooth. Add the arugula and toss until coated.

Spread each pita with 2 tablespoons of the mascarpone mixture. Divide the prosciutto on top. Divide the arugula and mound on top of the prosciutto. Carefully place a fried egg on top of each pita. Season the eggs with a pinch of salt and pepper, and serve.

savory polenta with sausage and dried cranberries

This is a total makeover for what can be ho-hum hot breakfast cereal. The polenta is like Southern grits, made creamy with Parmesan cheese, milk, and butter. Topped with sausage bits, dried cranberries, and a dollop of sweetened mascarpone cheese, this is my family's new favorite breakfast-for-dinner dish.

serves 4

2 cups low-sodium chicken broth
Kosher salt and freshly ground black pepper
1¼ cups polenta or yellow cornmeal
1 cup grated Parmesan cheese

¾ cup whole milk, at room temperature
5 tablespoons unsalted butter, cut into ½-inch pieces, at room temperature
1 tablespoon olive oil

1 pound pork sausage links, casings removed
1 cup (8 ounces) mascarpone cheese, at room temperature
3 tablespoons maple syrup or agave nectar
½ cup dried cranberries

In a heavy 5-quart saucepan, bring the chicken broth, 2½ cups water, and 1 tablespoon salt to a boil over medium-high heat. Gradually whisk in the polenta. Reduce the heat to low and cook, stirring often, until the mixture thickens and the cornmeal is tender, 15 to 20 minutes. Remove the pan from the heat.

Add the cheese, milk, and butter. Stir until the butter and cheese have melted. Season to taste with salt and pepper.

Meanwhile, in a large nonstick skillet, heat the oil over medium-high heat. Add the sausage. Using a wooden spoon, break up the sausage into ½-inch pieces. Cook until brown and fully cooked through, 8 to 10 minutes.

In a small bowl, whisk together the mascarpone cheese, maple syrup, and a pinch of salt until smooth.

Transfer the polenta to four bowls. Divide the sausage on top. Dollop with the mascarpone mixture and sprinkle with dried cranberries.

smoked salmon crostata

A crostata is an Italian tart that, in its simplest form, tends to be filled with jam or preserves, sometimes with fresh fruit or nuts. But over the years, the crostata has evolved into so much more. An easy preparation with the store-bought pie crust, this is a savory crostata that I like to serve at brunch, and now for dinner.

serves 8

1 (9-inch diameter) unroll-and-bake pie crust
2 ounces (¼ cup) fresh goat cheese, at room temperature
2 ounces (¼ cup) mascarpone cheese, at room temperature

8 ounces thinly sliced smoked salmon
1 tablespoon capers, rinsed, drained, and coarsely chopped

2 teaspoons chopped fresh chives
Grated zest of 1 large lemon

Preheat the oven to 450°F. Cut a piece of parchment paper to fit inside a 12 x 17-inch baking sheet and place on a work surface.

Form the dough into a ball with your hands and put it on the parchment paper (see Cook's Note). Roll the dough into an 11-inch circle, about ¼ inch thick. Using the tines of a fork, prick the dough all over. Lift the parchment paper and transfer to a baking sheet. Fold about 1 inch of the edge of the dough over itself, pleating the edge as you go, to form a 9-inch round. Bake until the crust is golden, 10 to 12 minutes. Allow the crust to cool completely, about 20 minutes.

In a small bowl, combine the goat cheese and mascarpone cheese. Spread the cheese mixture over the cooled crust. Top with the smoked salmon, capers, chives, and lemon zest. Cut into 8 wedges and serve.

cook's note

Rolling the dough into a ball first will soften it and make it more pliable and easier to roll into a larger circle.

baked potatoes with sausage and arugula

Next to eggs, potatoes and sausages are Todd's favorite breakfast foods. He grew up on baked potatoes. Here, instead of having them as a side dish, they're the star. A hearty topping of sausage, creamy tomato sauce, arugula, and Parmesan cheese turns it into meal. I go for turkey sausage in this, so it's not too heavy.

serves 4

4 (8- to 10-ounce) russet potatoes, pricked all over with a fork
3 tablespoons olive oil
1 small yellow onion, diced
Kosher salt and freshly ground black pepper
2 garlic cloves, minced

8 ounces sweet or spicy Italian-style turkey sausage, casings removed
1½ cups tomato-basil or marinara sauce
3 packed cups (3 ounces) baby arugula or spinach leaves

½ cup (4 ounces) mascarpone cheese, at room temperature
½ cup grated Parmesan cheese
2 tablespoons chopped fresh flat-leaf parsley leaves

Place an oven rack in the center of the oven. Preheat the oven to 350°F.

Wrap each potato in foil and bake for 1 hour, until tender when pierced with a knife. (Alternatively, cook the potatoes in a microwave. Put 2 potatoes at a time on a dinner plate; microwave on high for 8 minutes. Turn the potatoes over and cook for another 6 to 8 minutes, until soft. Repeat with the remaining potatoes.)

In a large skillet, heat the oil over medium-high heat. Add the onion, 1 teaspoon salt, and ½ teaspoon pepper. Cook, stirring frequently, until softened, about 3 minutes. Add the garlic and cook until aromatic, about 30 seconds. Add the sausage, and using a wooden spoon, break up the meat into ½-inch pieces. Cook until brown and cooked through, 6 to 8 minutes.

Add the marinara sauce and arugula. Bring the mixture to a boil and cook until the arugula has wilted, about 2 minutes. Stir in the mascarpone until the mixture forms a creamy sauce. Remove the pan from the heat and stir in the Parmesan cheese. Season to taste with salt and pepper.

Cut a slit in the top of each potato and gently squeeze the ends to form an opening in the top. Spoon the sausage sauce into each potato. Garnish with chopped parsley and serve.

veggies
& sides

veggies & sides

Fried Smashed Potatoes
with Lemon

Carrot and Yam Puree

Tomato-Basil Bread Pudding

Grilled Creamed Corn with
Spinach and Parmesan

Scallion and Mozzarella Cornbread

Red Potato and Tomato Salad

Roasted Zucchini and Summer Squash with Mint

Grilled Artichokes with Creamy Champagne Vinaigrette

Broccoli Rabe with Pecorino and Lemon

Sautéed Kale, Mushrooms, and Cranberries

Wilted Spinach with Tomatoes and Basil

Snap Pea and Edamame Sauté

fried smashed potatoes with lemon

Fried potatoes are my guilty pleasure, and these are no exception. This recipe requires you to boil the potatoes first so that they're soft enough to smash gently. This creates a flatter, larger surface area to fry, which means you get more crispy potato. Nothing wrong with that! The lemon juice, lemon zest, and herbs give these potatoes a freshness and slight acidity to cut through the richness. I can eat one after the other, after the other . . .

serves 4

2 pounds baby or fingerling potatoes
¼ cup plus 3 tablepoons extra-virgin olive oil, plus more as needed
3 garlic cloves, peeled and halved

Grated zest of 2 lemons
3 tablespoons fresh lemon juice
2 tablespoons chopped fresh flat-leaf parsley leaves
1 tablespoon chopped fresh thyme leaves

½ teaspoon kosher salt
½ teaspoon freshly ground black pepper

Put the potatoes in an 8-quart pot with enough salted cold water to cover by at least 2 inches. Bring the water to a boil and cook until the potatoes are tender, 20 to 25 minutes. Drain the potatoes in a colander and allow to dry for 5 minutes. Using the palm of your hand, gently press the potatoes until lightly smashed.

In a large, nonstick skillet, heat ¼ cup of the oil over medium-high heat. Add the garlic and cook until fragrant and lightly brown, about 1 minute. Remove the garlic and discard. In batches, add the potatoes and cook, without stirring, for 5 to 8 minutes, until the bottoms turn golden brown. Using a spatula, turn the potatoes over and cook, drizzling with oil if needed, for 5 to 8 minutes longer, until golden brown on the underside. Transfer to a serving bowl once cooked.

In a small bowl, whisk together the remaining 3 tablespoons oil, the lemon zest, lemon juice, parsley, thyme, salt, and pepper.

Spoon the dressing over the potatoes and toss gently until coated. Season to taste with salt and pepper, and serve.

carrot and yam puree

When Jade was a baby, I made all of her food at home, and this puree was one of her favorites. But she had to share it with me since it was one of my favorites, too! Even now that Jade has outgrown baby food, I still make this recipe and serve it with fish, like Broiled Tilapia with Mustard-Chive Sauce (page 133). There are some things Jade and I will never outgrow.

serves 4 to 6

⅓ cup olive oil
1 large onion, diced
3 garlic cloves, minced

2 pounds carrots, peeled and
   thinly sliced
2 pounds yams, peeled and cut
   into ¾-inch pieces

Kosher salt and freshly ground
   black pepper
4 cups low-sodium chicken
   broth

In a saucepan or Dutch oven, heat the oil over medium-high heat. Add the onion and cook until tender, about 5 minutes. Add the garlic and cook for 1 minute, until aromatic. Add the carrots, yams, 1 teaspoon salt, and ½ teaspoon pepper. Cook for 5 minutes, until slightly softened. Pour in the broth and ½ cup water, and bring to a boil. Reduce the heat and simmer until the carrots and yams are tender, about 25 minutes.

Using a ladle, remove 2 cups of the cooking liquid and reserve. Using an immersion blender (see Cook's Note), puree the mixture until slightly chunky, adding the reserved cooking liquid, ¼ cup at a time, if needed. Season to taste with salt and pepper.

cook's note

The carrot-yam mixture can also be drained in a colander (remember to reserve the cooking liquid!) and, working in batches, blended in a food processor or blender.

tomato-basil bread pudding

Sweet or savory, bread puddings are definitely a treat. For maximum flavor, I opt for a multigrain bread. Combined with fresh tomatoes and fragrant basil, this makes a great side dish or even vegetarian main course.

serves 4 as a main course or 6 to 8 as a side dish

Butter, for the baking dish
½ (8-ounce) multigrain loaf, cut into ½-inch cubes
⅓ cup olive oil
1 large or 2 small shallots, thinly sliced
2 garlic cloves, minced

1 pint cherry or grape tomatoes, halved
Kosher salt and freshly ground black pepper
1 packed cup chopped fresh basil

1½ cups grated Parmesan cheese
7 large eggs, at room temperature
1 cup whole milk

Place an oven rack in the center of the oven. Preheat the oven to 375°F.

Butter a 9 x 13 x 2-inch glass baking dish. Add the bread cubes and set aside.

In a large skillet, heat the oil over medium-high heat. Add the shallots and garlic. Cook, stirring constantly, for 1 minute until fragrant. Add the tomatoes, 1 teaspoon salt, and ¼ teaspoon pepper. Cook for 2 minutes, until slightly soft. Remove the pan from the heat and stir in the basil.

Pour the tomato mixture over the bread cubes, add the Parmesan, and combine well.

In a large bowl, beat the eggs, milk, 1 teaspoon salt, and ½ teaspoon pepper until smooth. Pour the custard over the bread mixture and gently toss to coat.

Bake for 25 to 30 minutes, until slightly puffed and golden. Cool for 5 minutes. Cut into wedges and serve.

grilled creamed corn with spinach and parmesan

I've always been a fan of creamed corn but never the canned kind because of the additives and preservatives. For a fresh take on the same dish, I grill the corn first so that the heat tenderizes the kernels while at the same time giving them a slight char and a smoky flavor. I add spinach so there's a semblance of creamed spinach, too. Two dishes in one!

serves 4

6 ears corn, husks and silks removed
3 tablespoons unsalted butter, at room temperature

Kosher salt and freshly ground black pepper
1 tablespoon flour
¾ cup heavy cream

⅔ cup whole milk
⅓ cup grated Parmesan cheese
1 (6-ounce) bag of fresh spinach

Heat a grill pan over medium-high heat or preheat a gas or charcoal grill.

Grill the corn, turning every 5 to 6 minutes, until tender, about 15 minutes. When cool enough to handle, remove the kernels.

In a large, high-sided skillet, heat the butter over medium-high heat. Add the corn and season with salt and pepper. Cook for 3 minutes, until softened. Stir in the flour and cook for 1 minute. Reduce the heat to medium and add the cream. Simmer for 2 to 3 minutes, until the mixture thickens.

Pour half of the mixture into a food processor. Blend until smooth. Pour the pureed mixture back into the skillet and add the milk, Parmesan cheese, and spinach. Cook over low heat until the spinach has wilted and the mixture is warmed through, about 5 minutes. Season to taste with salt and pepper, and serve.

scallion and mozzarella cornbread

I use cornbread in my Thanksgiving stuffing and for croutons, and I serve it on its own as long as it's not boring or bland. Adding scallions, green olives stuffed with pimientos, and mozzarella cheese ensures that this cornbread will be neither boring nor bland. Every bite will pop with unexpected flavor.

serves 4 to 6

Vegetable oil cooking spray
2 (8.5-ounce) boxes cornbread
   mix, such as Jiffy
½ cup buttermilk, at room
   temperature
3 tablespoons unsalted butter,
   melted

2 large eggs, at room
   temperature
10 large pimiento-stuffed green
   olives, coarsely chopped
   (½ cup)

5 scallions, white and pale green
   parts only, finely chopped
   (½ cup)
1 cup (4 ounces) shredded
   mozzarella cheese

Place an oven rack in the center of the oven. Preheat the oven to 400°F. Spray an 8-inch square glass baking dish with vegetable oil. Line the bottom and sides of the baking dish with two pieces of parchment, each 7 inches wide and 15 inches long, allowing the excess parchment to overhang the sides.

In a medium bowl, mix the cornbread mix, buttermilk, melted butter, eggs, olives, scallions, and cheese until the mixture forms a thick, lumpy batter. Using a spatula, spread the batter into the prepared baking dish. Bake for 25 to 30 minutes, until golden brown. Allow the cornbread to cool in the pan for 15 minutes.

Using the excess parchment as handles, remove the cornbread from the pan. Peel away the parchment and cut the cornbread into 1½-inch squares.

red potato and tomato salad

The ingredients couldn't be any simpler yet the taste is anything but. The natural juices from the tomatoes, capers, and olives along with rich extra-virgin olive oil are absorbed into the potatoes, allowing the flavors to meld and develop as the salad sits. If you have time, let it marinate in the refrigerator for half an hour before serving; toss well before setting on the table.

serves 4

1 pound baby red potatoes, halved
1 pint cherry tomatoes, halved
3 scallions, white and pale green parts, thinly sliced
⅓ cup pitted black olives, halved

⅓ cup chopped fresh flat-leaf parsley leaves
2 tablespoons capers, rinsed and drained
1 tablespoon chopped fresh thyme leaves

¼ cup extra-virgin olive oil
Grated zest of 1 large lemon
Kosher salt and freshly ground black pepper

Put the potatoes in a medium saucepan with enough salted cold water to cover by at least 2 inches. Bring the water to a boil and cook until the potatoes are tender, 15 to 20 minutes. Drain the potatoes in a colander and allow to dry for 5 minutes.

In a serving bowl, combine the potatoes, tomatoes, scallions, olives, parsley, capers, thyme, olive oil, and lemon zest. Toss gently until all ingredients are coated. Season to taste with salt and pepper.

roasted zucchini and summer squash with mint

A beautiful, colorful blend of roasted squash, onions, and garlic tossed with fresh mint is an ideal side dish for almost any main course. Eating your vegetables in this case tastes so good.

serves 4

Vegetable oil cooking spray
3 medium zucchini
3 medium yellow summer squash
1 leek, white and pale green
  part only, cut crosswise into
  ½-inch-thick rings and rinsed

2 garlic cloves, chopped
3 tablespoons extra-virgin
  olive oil
1½ teaspoons kosher salt

½ teaspoon freshly ground
  black pepper
¼ cup chopped fresh mint
  leaves

Preheat the oven to 425°F. Place an oven rack in the upper third of the oven. Spray a heavy baking sheet with vegetable oil.

Trim the zucchini and squash, and then cut each one in half lengthwise. Cut the halves crosswise into 1-inch half-moons.

Arrange the zucchini, squash, leek, and garlic in a single layer on the prepared baking sheet. Drizzle with 2 tablespoons of the olive oil. Bake for 10 minutes. Turn the vegetables over and continue to bake for 5 minutes longer.

Transfer the vegetables to a platter and season with the salt and pepper. Add the mint and toss to combine. Drizzle with the remaining tablespoon oil and serve.

grilled artichokes with creamy champagne vinaigrette

I love fresh artichokes, but preparing them can be time-consuming. I cut out that step entirely and instead take advantage of frozen artichoke hearts to get an equally scrumptious dish, made special with a hint of rosemary, the char of the grill, and a unique, creamy champagne vinaigrette.

serves 4

⅓ cup plus ¼ cup extra-virgin olive oil
1 tablespoon chopped fresh rosemary leaves
2 garlic cloves, minced

Kosher salt and freshly ground black pepper
1 pound frozen artichoke hearts, thawed
½ cup crème fraîche

2 tablespoons champagne vinegar
2 tablespoons honey

In a medium bowl, whisk together ⅓ cup of the oil, the rosemary, garlic, 1 teaspoon salt, and ¼ teaspoon pepper. Add the artichokes and toss until coated.

Heat a grill pan over medium-high heat or preheat a gas or charcoal grill. Grill the artichokes for 1 to 2 minutes on each side, until lightly charred. Transfer to a serving bowl and set aside to cool slightly.

In a medium bowl, whisk together the crème fraîche, remaining ¼ cup olive oil, the vinegar, honey, ½ teaspoon salt, and ¼ teaspoon pepper until smooth. Serve the vinaigrette alongside the artichokes as a dipping sauce.

broccoli rabe with pecorino and lemon

Broccoli rabe is a favorite Italian winter vegetable that is so simple to make, I often have it at my dinner table. It has a distinct but slight bitterness which is offset by lemon and tamed by pecorino in this recipe.

serves 4

1 pound broccoli rabe (rapini) or baby broccoli, ends trimmed and tough stems peeled
⅓ cup extra-virgin olive oil

¼ cup lemon juice (from 1 large lemon)
½ teaspoon crushed red pepper flakes (optional)
¾ teaspoon kosher salt

¼ teaspoon freshly ground black pepper
⅔ cup grated pecorino romano cheese

Bring a large pot of salted water to a boil over medium-high heat. Add the broccoli rabe and cook until just tender but still bright green, 3 to 5 minutes. Drain well and transfer to a serving bowl.

In a medium bowl, whisk together the oil, lemon juice, pepper flakes if using, the salt, and pepper. Pour the sauce over the broccoli rabe, add the cheese, and toss until coated.

sautéed kale, mushrooms, and cranberries

Kale is a hearty, leafy green that I use often in soups and stews, and even bake in the oven to turn into crispy chips. Here, I sauté it with sweet-tart dried cranberries and meaty mushrooms to make a good, and good for you, vegetable dish that you can enjoy by itself, with a simply cooked piece of halibut or chicken breast, or over rice or pasta, such as orzo.

serves 4

2 tablespoons unsalted butter, at room temperature
1 tablespoon olive oil
1 large or 2 small shallots, thinly sliced

1 medium leek, white and pale green parts only, thinly sliced and rinsed
8 ounces cremini or button mushrooms, sliced (4 cups)
Kosher salt and freshly ground black pepper

12 ounces kale, stemmed and coarsely chopped
¼ cup low-sodium chicken or vegetable broth
⅓ cup dried cranberries

In a large skillet, heat the butter and oil over medium-high heat. Add the shallots, leek, mushrooms, 1½ teaspoons salt, and ½ teaspoon pepper. Cook, stirring frequently, until the vegetables are soft, about 8 minutes. Add the kale and cook until wilted, about 6 minutes. Add the broth and cranberries. Bring to a boil and scrape up the browned bits that cling to the bottom of the pan with a wooden spoon. Season to taste with salt and pepper, and serve.

wilted spinach with tomatoes and basil

Quick veggie sautés should be in everyone's weeknight meal repertoire. Simple spinach greens become so much more flavorful with shallots, garlic, basil, and juicy bursts of cherry tomatoes. With a dish so easy and tasty, there's no reason not to eat your vegetables.

serves 4

3 tablespoons olive oil
1 large or 2 small shallots, thinly
    sliced
2 garlic cloves, chopped
1 pint cherry tomatoes, halved

1 pound fresh spinach leaves
½ teaspoon kosher salt
½ teaspoon freshly ground
    black pepper

¼ cup balsamic vinegar
⅓ cup chopped fresh basil
    leaves

In a large skillet, heat the oil over medium-high heat. Add the shallots and cook for 2 to 3 minutes, until soft. Add the garlic and cook for 30 seconds, until aromatic. Add the tomatoes and cook for 2 minutes. In batches, add the spinach and cook until wilted, about 5 minutes. Season with the salt and pepper. Stir in the balsamic vinegar and basil. Simmer for 1 minute and serve.

snap pea and edamame sauté

This dish literally takes fewer than seven minutes to cook. I love it alongside Balsamic-Glazed Salmon (page 132). The colors are beautiful together.

serves 4

2 tablespoons olive oil
1 large or 2 small shallots, thinly
    sliced
2 garlic cloves, minced

2 cups (10 ounces) shelled
    edamame
2½ cups (8 ounces) sugar snap
    peas, halved

½ teaspoon kosher salt
¼ teaspoon freshly ground
    black pepper

In a medium skillet, heat the oil over medium-high heat. Add the shallots and cook until soft, about 3 minutes. Add the garlic and cook until aromatic, about 30 seconds. Add the edamame, snap peas, salt, and pepper and cook for 3 minutes, until warmed through.

desserts

desserts

Peanut Butter Cookies with Blackberry Jam

Oatmeal, Cranberry, and
Chocolate Chunk Cookies

Spiced Apple Walnut Cupcakes

Mini Pumpkin Cupcakes
with Chocolate Frosting

Chocolate Mascarpone Pound Cake

Double Chocolate and Espresso Cookies

Chocolate-Hazelnut Drop Cookies

Apricot Oat Bars

Raspberry-Balsamic Parfaits

Gingerbread Affogato

peanut butter cookies with blackberry jam

For me, a meal isn't complete without a bite of something sweet. These cookies are a take on the classic peanut butter and jelly combo; a little bit of cocoa powder creates that beloved peanut-butter-and-chocolate combination, too.

makes 10 (4-inch) cookies

1 cup all-purpose flour
⅓ cup unsweetened cocoa powder
½ teaspoon baking soda
⅛ teaspoon fine sea salt

8 tablespoons (1 stick) unsalted butter, cut into ½-inch pieces, at room temperature
¾ cup creamy peanut butter, at room temperature
1 cup granulated sugar

½ packed cup light brown sugar
1 large egg, beaten, at room temperature
1 teaspoon pure vanilla extract
¼ cup blackberry jam

Place an oven rack in the center of the oven. Preheat the oven to 375°F. Line two baking sheets with parchment.

In a medium bowl, sift together the flour, cocoa powder, baking soda, and salt.

In a stand mixer fitted with the paddle attachment, beat the butter, peanut butter, ¾ cup of the granulated sugar, and all the light brown sugar, scraping down the side of the bowl as needed, until smooth, about 30 seconds. Add the egg and vanilla, and mix until blended. With the machine running on low speed, gradually add the flour mixture and mix until just incorporated.

Put the remaining ¼ cup granulated sugar into a small bowl. Form the dough into ¼-cup balls and roll in the sugar. Arrange 5 balls of dough, evenly apart, on each baking sheet. Using a round ¼-teaspoon measure, or the thin end of a wooden spoon, make an indentation in the center of each ball of dough, about ½ to ¾ inch deep. Spoon 1 teaspoon of jam into each depression.

Bake the cookies for 11 to 14 minutes, until the dough has spread and the surface of the cookies is crackled. Cool for 5 minutes and then transfer to a wire rack to cool completely, about 20 minutes.

oatmeal, cranberry, and chocolate chunk cookies

Todd, Jade, and I joined my friend Olympic figure skater Brian Boitano for an outing at the ice-skating rink in downtown Los Angeles. I baked these cookies, packed them up, and brought them with us. The mixture of sweetened, tart cranberries with chunks of chocolate is heavenly. You can definitely use chocolate chips if you prefer, but I like the homemade look of roughly chopped chocolate and the chunks give you bigger, gooier bites of chocolate.

makes 12 cookies

1 cup all-purpose flour
¾ teaspoon ground cinnamon
½ teaspoon baking powder
½ teaspoon baking soda
½ teaspoon fine sea salt
8 tablespoons (1 stick) unsalted
   butter, at room temperature

½ cup light brown sugar
½ cup granulated sugar
1 large egg, at room
   temperature
½ teaspoon pure vanilla extract
2 cups old-fashioned rolled
   oats

1 cup dried cranberries
1 (4-ounce) 60% cacao
   bittersweet chocolate bar,
   such as Ghirardelli, chopped
   into ¼-inch chunks

Place an oven rack in the center of the oven. Preheat the oven to 350°F. Line two baking sheets with parchment paper.

In a medium bowl, whisk together the flour, cinnamon, baking powder, baking soda, and salt.

In a stand mixer fitted with a paddle attachment, beat the butter and sugars together until light and fluffy, about 1 minute. Add the egg and vanilla and beat until smooth. With the machine running, gradually add the flour mixture. Add the oats, cranberries, and chocolate chunks. Mix until just incorporated; it will be stiff.

Using a 4-ounce cookie scoop or ¼-cup measure, scoop 12 (2-inch) slightly rounded mounds of the dough. Place 6 balls of dough, spaced evenly apart, on each baking sheet. Using the back of a spoon, flatten the tops slightly.

Bake for 13 to 15 minutes, until the cookies are slightly golden on the edges. Allow the cookies to cool on the baking sheet for 20 minutes.

spiced apple walnut cupcakes

This recipe started out as a Thanksgiving loaf cake with all of the flavors of the holidays in it—pumpkin pie spice mix, apples, and maple syrup. Everyone fell in love with it, especially Jade. So I turned this into cupcakes, which bake quickly and are lots of fun for Jade to eat. The frosting is optional; these are great with or without, and I make them both ways.

makes 20 cupcakes

cupcakes

3 medium green apples, such as Granny Smith, peeled, cored, and diced into ¼-inch pieces
1½ cups maple syrup
3 large eggs, at room temperature
¾ packed cup light brown sugar
¾ cup vegetable oil

1 tablespoon pure vanilla extract
3 cups all-purpose flour
1½ teaspoons baking powder
1½ teaspoons baking soda
1½ tablespoons pumpkin pie spice
½ teaspoon fine sea salt
1 cup chopped walnuts

frosting

4 cups confectioners' sugar
8 ounces cream cheese, at room temperature
3 tablespoons heavy cream, at room temperature
1 tablespoon pure vanilla extract

for the cupcakes: Place an oven rack in the center of the oven. Preheat the oven to 350°F. Line 20 muffin cups with paper liners.

In a large bowl, mix the apples, maple syrup, eggs, sugar, oil, and vanilla. In a separate medium bowl, whisk together the flour, baking powder, baking soda, pumpkin pie spice, and salt. In batches, mix the dry ingredients into the apple mixture. Stir in the walnuts.

Spoon ⅓-cup portions of the batter into the muffin cups and bake for 20 to 22 minutes, until the cupcakes are light golden and a tester inserted into them comes out clean. Cool the cupcakes on a wire rack.

for the frosting: In a medium bowl, combine the confectioners' sugar, cream cheese, cream, and vanilla. Using an electric mixer, beat on low speed until smooth. Increase the speed to high and beat until light and fluffy, about 1 minute.

Using a small spatula, spread the frosting on top of the cupcakes.

mini pumpkin cupcakes with chocolate frosting

Halloween is all about candy, costumes, and pumpkins—and not just carved. I made these mini cupcakes for a pre–trick-or-treat gathering and they were a hit with both the kids and the adults. The chocolate frosting is decadent and an ideal canvas for the kids to decorate to their hearts' content.

makes 48 mini cupcakes

cupcakes

1 (15-ounce) can of 100% pure pumpkin, such as Libby's
2 cups vanilla cake mix, such as Betty Crocker Super Moist French Vanilla
¼ cup vegetable oil
2 tablespoons whole milk
2 large eggs, at room temperature
2¼ teaspoons pumpkin pie spice

frosting

1½ cups confectioners' sugar
¾ cup (6 ounces) cream cheese, at room temperature
6 tablespoons (¾ stick) unsalted butter, at room temperature
¾ cup unsweetened cocoa powder
⅓ cup sour cream
Mini-chocolate chips, sprinkles, colored sugar, and small candies, for decorating

for the cupcakes: Place an oven rack in the center of the oven. Preheat the oven to 350°F. Line 48 mini-muffin molds with paper liners. (See Cook's Note.)

In a large bowl, combine the pumpkin, cake mix, oil, milk, eggs, and pumpkin pie spice. Using an electric mixer, beat the mixture on low speed until smooth. Increase the speed to high and beat for 2 minutes, until light and fluffy.

Using a small ice cream scoop or a spoon, fill the prepared molds with the batter. Bake for 10 to 12 minutes, until puffed and golden. Cool in the pan for 10 minutes. Transfer to a wire rack to cool completely before frosting, about 20 minutes.

for the frosting: In a medium bowl, combine the confectioners' sugar, cream cheese, butter, cocoa powder, and sour cream. Using an electric mixer, beat on low speed until smooth. Increase the speed to high and beat until light and fluffy, about 1 minute.

Using a small spatula, spread the frosting on top of the cupcakes. Decorate as desired.

cook's note

The batter can also be spooned into 16 regular-sized cupcake molds and baked at 350°F for 20 to 25 minutes.

chocolate mascarpone pound cake

Admittedly, my whole family has a sweet tooth—I just have the biggest! My mom was always very creative, coming up with desserts and ways to use the ingredients we had in the house. She'd make a pound cake similar to this and drizzle it with an espresso icing. But I've changed it a bit, finishing it with a more kid-friendly chocolate glaze.

makes 1 (9-inch) loaf cake

cake

Butter, for the pan
Flour, for the pan
1 (16-ounce) box of pound cake
    mix, such as Betty Crocker
⅓ cup unsweetened cocoa
    powder, such as Hershey's
4 tablespoons (½ stick) unsalted
    butter, at room temperature

¼ cup (2 ounces) mascarpone
    cheese, at room temperature
⅔ cup whole milk
3 tablespoons vegetable oil
2 large eggs, at room
    temperature
1 teaspoon pure vanilla extract

glaze

1½ cups confectioners' sugar
¼ cup unsweetened cocoa
    powder, such as Hershey's
1 teaspoon pure vanilla extract

for the cake: Place an oven rack in the center of the oven. Preheat the oven to 350°F. Butter and flour a 9 x 5-inch metal loaf pan.

In a large bowl, combine the pound cake mix, cocoa powder, butter, mascarpone cheese, milk, vegetable oil, eggs, and vanilla extract. Using an electric mixer, beat on low speed for 30 seconds. Increase the speed to medium and beat for 2 minutes until smooth and thick.

Pour the batter into the prepared pan. Bake for 50 to 55 minutes, until a cake tester inserted into the middle of the cake comes out clean. Cool for 10 minutes and invert onto a rack to cool completely, about 1 hour.

for the glaze: In a small bowl, whisk together the sugar and cocoa powder. Add the vanilla and slowly whisk in 3 tablespoons water, or a little more as needed, until the mixture is thick. Spoon the glaze over the cake and serve.

double chocolate and espresso cookies

This cookie combines two of my all-time loves: chocolate and espresso. It's actually a quadruple dose of chocolate with the cocoa powder, melted chocolate, the chocolate-covered espresso beans, and the chocolate chips. Pure decadence.

makes 10 to 12 (3-inch) cookies

⅓ cup dark chocolate–covered espresso beans
1 cup all-purpose flour
2 tablespoons unsweetened cocoa powder
1 teaspoon baking powder
¼ teaspoon fine sea salt

2 tablespoons unsalted butter, at room temperature
6 ounces semi-sweet chocolate, such as Ghirardelli, chopped into ½-inch pieces
¾ cup sugar

2 large eggs, at room temperature
1 teaspoon pure vanilla extract
1 cup semi-sweet chocolate chips, such as Nestlé Toll House

Place an oven rack in the center of the oven. Preheat the oven to 300°F. Line two baking sheets with parchment.

In the bowl of a food processor, finely chop the chocolate-covered espresso beans. In a medium bowl, whisk together the chopped espresso beans, the flour, cocoa powder, baking powder, and salt.

Put the butter and chocolate in a microwave-safe bowl. Microwave on medium power (50%) for 1 minute and 30 seconds. Stir and microwave on medium power (50%) for 1 minute. Stir until the chocolate is fully melted and smooth; the mixture will be thick.

In another medium bowl, whisk together the sugar, eggs, 2 tablespoons water, and the vanilla. Gradually add the dry ingredients and stir until thick and smooth. Fold in the melted chocolate. Stir in the chocolate chips.

Using a cookie or ice cream scoop, scoop level ¼-cup balls of the batter onto the prepared baking sheets, spacing them 2 inches apart. Bake for 18 to 20 minutes, until slightly puffed and the tops begin to crack. Allow the cookies to cool completely on the baking sheets.

chocolate-hazelnut drop cookies

Similar to my family's Italian wedding cookies (which are a lot like the Mexican kind), these drop cookies get their flavor from the smooth, velvety combination of melted chocolate and hazelnuts—also known as gianduja. This is the stuff that makes my mouth water and brings me back to my childhood. Just as with chocolate chip cookies, some people like theirs soft and other people like them crispy. For softer cookies, bake them for ten minutes; for firmer ones, give them the full twelve minutes in the oven.

makes 36 cookies

16 tablespoons (2 sticks) butter, at room temperature
1¼ cups confectioners' sugar

1 teaspoon pure vanilla extract
2 cups all-purpose flour

½ cup chocolate-hazelnut spread, such as Nutella, at room temperature

Place an oven rack in the center of the oven. Preheat the oven to 350°F. Line three baking sheets with parchment.

In an electric mixer fitted with the paddle attachment, beat the butter and ¼ cup of the sugar on high speed until light and fluffy, 2 to 3 minutes. Beat in the vanilla. With the machine running on low speed, gradually add the flour and mix just until incorporated. Beat in the chocolate-hazelnut spread.

Roll the dough into 36 (1½-inch) balls and place 12 balls of dough on each baking sheet. Bake for 10 to 12 minutes, until the bottoms of the cookies flatten out slightly. Cool for 5 minutes and transfer to a wire rack to cool completely, about 30 minutes.

Put the remaining 1 cup sugar in a medium bowl. In batches, roll the cookies in the sugar until coated. Store in an airtight container at room temperature.

apricot oat bars

I had oat bars similar to these when I went to Gualala, in northern California, for a friend's wedding. They were so good, I went to the bakery that made them every single morning to buy one. You can use any kind of jam and fruit in this recipe. Whatever your preference, they're easy to make and promise to be a dessert you'll make over and over again.

makes 24 (2½-inch) bars

Vegetable oil cooking spray
1 (13-ounce) jar apricot jam or
    preserves (about 1¼ cups)
8 dried apricots, chopped into
    ¼-inch pieces (about ⅓ cup)
1¾ cups all-purpose flour
1 packed cup light brown sugar

1 teaspoon ground cinnamon
¾ teaspoon fine sea salt
¾ teaspoon baking soda
1¾ cups old-fashioned rolled
    oats
1 cup (4 ounces) coarsely
    chopped walnuts

16 tablespoons (2 sticks)
    unsalted butter, melted
1 large egg, beaten, at room
    temperature
1 teaspoon pure vanilla extract

Place an oven rack in the center of the oven. Preheat the oven to 350°F. Spray a 9 x 13 x 2-inch metal baking dish with vegetable oil. Line the bottom and sides of the pan with parchment. Spray the parchment with vegetable oil.

In a small bowl, mix the jam and apricots.

In a large bowl, whisk together the flour, sugar, cinnamon, salt, and baking soda. Stir in the oats and walnuts. Add the butter, egg, and vanilla and stir until incorporated.

Using a fork or clean fingers, lightly press half of the crust mixture onto the bottom of the prepared pan. Using a spatula, spread the filling over the crust, leaving a ½-inch border around the edge of the pan. Cover the filling with the remaining crust mixture and gently press to flatten.

Bake for 30 to 35 minutes, until light golden. Cool for 30 minutes to 1 hour. Cut into bars and store in an airtight container for up to 3 days.

raspberry-balsamic parfaits

Parfaits can be so many variations of flavors and textures and are always so beautiful with their colorful layers. These sweet-tart-creamy raspberry-balsamic ones can be whipped up in a snap. I love the sweet crunch the sugar candy adds. This dessert makes for a wonderfully fresh finish to a weeknight meal.

serves 4

Vegetable oil cooking spray
2 cups (8 ounces) fresh
    raspberries
3 tablespoons aged balsamic
    vinegar (aged for 5 to 10 years)

⅓ cup turbinado sugar, such as
    Sugar in the Raw
1 cup (8 ounces) mascarpone
    cheese, at room temperature

¼ cup sour cream, at room
    temperature
3 tablespoons honey

Line a small baking sheet with parchment or wax paper and spray with vegetable oil.

In a small bowl, carefully toss the raspberries and vinegar together. Let stand for 15 minutes.

Heat a 10-inch nonstick skillet over medium heat. Add the sugar and cook, stirring occasionally, until it melts, about 5 minutes. Pour the sugar onto the prepared baking sheet and allow to cool, 5 to 10 minutes. When cool enough to handle, crumble into small pieces.

In another small bowl, mix the mascarpone cheese, sour cream, and honey until smooth.

Spoon the raspberry mixture into 4 (8-ounce) glasses. Dollop the mascarpone mixture on top. Sprinkle with the crumbled sugar and serve.

gingerbread affogato

When you're craving a cup of coffee at the end of the meal, try this recipe, which makes something a little more special. I incorporate the flavors of a gingerbread cookie—ginger, cinnamon, and cloves—into a simple syrup used to sweeten hot espresso doused with hazelnut liqueur. Then I pour it over a scoop of vanilla gelato for a true Italian treat.

serves 4

1½ cups sugar
1 (1-inch) piece of fresh ginger, thinly sliced
2 cinnamon sticks

3 whole cloves
1 tablespoon instant espresso powder

1 to 2 tablespoons hazelnut liqueur, such as Frangelico (optional)
1 pint vanilla gelato or ice cream

In a small saucepan, combine 1 cup water, the sugar, ginger, cinnamon, and cloves over medium heat. Bring to a boil, reduce the heat, and simmer, stirring occasionally, for 5 minutes or until the sugar has dissolved. Take the pan off the heat and allow the syrup to cool, about 20 minutes. Remove the ginger, cinnamon, and cloves and discard.

Bring ½ cup water to a boil and pour into a 1-cup glass measuring cup. Whisk in the espresso powder and liqueur, if using, until the powder is dissolved.

Scoop the gelato into four dessert bowls or glasses. Pour ¼ cup of the ginger syrup and 2 tablespoons espresso over each. Serve immediately.

acknowledgments

As a busy working mother, I rely on a trusted team to assist me in getting my recipes from my personal handwritten notebook pages to a final beautiful cookbook for all to enjoy. From the artful photography to the inspiring, fresh layout, this book would not exist without the endless talent from these people.

A huge thank you to photographer Amy Neunsinger, who opened her home—and closet—to me, creating an atmosphere of peace, warmth, and inspiration. You and your assistants, Andy Mitchell, Shawn Miller, and Hector Prida, are artists through and through. To my meticulous recipe-testing gurus, Sandra Tripicchio, Andy Sheen-Turner, and Diana Bassett, my gratitude for your unparalleled culinary prowess. For your guidance in bringing this book to life, I thank Rica Allannic, Marysarah Quinn, and Kate Tyler at Clarkson Potter.

Kyle Schuneman, for your keen eye for style and embracing my "less is more" philosophy so seamlessly, and the tireless Valerie Aikman-Smith, for gorgeous food styling. Julie Morgan, I cherish our early-morning beauty sessions; you work magic every day.

For your continued dedication and support: Jon Rosen, Suzanne Gluck, Eric Greenspan, and Jocelyn Hayes. I am one lucky gal to have you all on my side.

To my dear family, what a fabulous journey this has been so far. . . . Here's to seeing what's in store for us next.

Looking forward to sitting down with Todd and Jade at the dinner table tonight, my favorite place on earth!

credits

Viking
Le Creuset

index

Note: Page references in *italics* indicate photographs.

238 index

monday

tuesday

wednesday

thursday

friday